Britain in Afghanistan

2. The Second Afghan War
1878-80

Britain in Afghanistan

2. The Second Afghan War
1878-80

Archibald Forbes

LEONAUR

Britain in Afghanistan 2: the Second Afghan War 1878-80
by Archibald Forbes

Published by Leonaur Ltd

ISBN: 978-1-84677-306-8 (hardcover)
ISBN: 978-1-84677-305-1 (softcover)

http://www.leonaur.com

Publisher's Notes

In the interests of authenticity, the spellings, grammar and place names used have been retained from the original editions.

The opinions of the authors represent a view of events in which he was a participant related from his own perspective, as such the text is relevant as an historical document.

The views expressed in this book are not necessarily those of the publisher.

Contents

CHAPTER 1

The First Campaign

A brief period of peace intervened between the ratification of the treaty of Gundamuk on May 30th, 1879, and the renewal of hostilities consequent on the massacre at Cabul of Sir Louis Cavagnari and the whole entourage of the mission of which he was the head. There was nothing identical or even similar in the motives of the two campaigns, and regarded purely on principle they might be regarded as two distinct wars, rather than as successive campaigns of one and the same war. But the interval between them was so short that the ink of the signatures to the treaty of Gundamuk may be said to have been scarcely dry when the murder of the British Envoy tore that document into bloody shreds; and it seems the simplest and most convenient method to designate the two years of hostilities from November 1878 to September 1880, as the 'Second Afghan War,' notwithstanding the three months' interval of peace in the summer of 1879.

Dost Mahomed died in 1863, and after a long struggle his son Shere Ali possessed himself of the throne bequeathed to him by his father. The relations between Shere Ali and the successive Viceroys of India were friendly, although not close. The consistent aim of the British policy was to maintain Afghanistan in the position of a strong, friendly, and independent state, prepared in certain contingencies to co-operate in keeping at a distance foreign intrigue or aggression; and while this object was promoted by donations of money and arms, to abstain from interference in the internal affairs of the country, while according a friendly recognition to the successive occupants of its throne, without undertaking indefinite liabilities in their interest. The aim, in a word, was to utilise Afghanistan as a 'buffer' state between the northwestern frontier of British India and Russian advances from the direction of Central Asia. Shere Ali was never a very comfortable ally; he was of a saturnine and suspicious nature, and he seems also to have had an overweening sense of the value of the position of Afghanistan, interposed between two great powers profoundly jealous one of the other. He did not succeed with Lord Northbrook in an attempt to work on that Viceroy by playing off the bogey of Russian aggression; and as the consequence of this failure he allowed himself to display marked evidences of disaffected feeling. Cognisance was taken of this 'attitude of extreme reserve,' and early in 1876 Lord Lytton arrived in India charged with instructions to break away from the policy designated as that of 'masterly inactivity,' and to initiate a new basis of relations with Afghanistan and its Ameer.

Lord Lytton's instructions directed him to despatch without delay a mission to Cabul, whose errand would be to require of the Ameer the acceptance of a permanent Resident and free access to the frontier positions of Afghanistan on the part of British officers, who should have opportunity of conferring with the Ameer on matters of common interest with 'becoming attention to their friendly councils.' Those were demands notoriously obnoxious to the Afghan monarch and the Afghan people. Compliance with them involved sacrifice of independence, and the Afghan loathing of Feringhee officials in their midst had been fiercely evinced in the long bloody struggle and awful catastrophe recorded in earlier pages of this volume. Probably the Ameer, had he desired, would not have dared to concede such demands on any terms, no matter how full of advantage. But the terms which Lord Lytton was instructed to tender as an equivalent were strangely meagre. The Ameer was to receive a money gift, and a precarious stipend regarding which the new Viceroy was to 'deem it inconvenient to commit his government to any permanent pecuniary obligation.' The desiderated recognition of Abdoolah Jan as Shere Ali's successor was promised with the qualifying reservation that the promise 'did not imply or necessitate any intervention in the internal affairs of the state.' The guarantee against foreign aggression was vague and indefinite, and the Government of India reserved to itself entire 'freedom of judgment as to the character of circumstances involving the obligation of material support.'

The Ameer replied to the notice that a mission was about to proceed to Cabul by a courteous declinature to receive an Envoy, assigning several specious reasons. He was quite satisfied with the existing friendly relations, and desired no change in them; he could not guarantee the safety of the Envoy and his people; if he admitted a British mission, he would have no excuse for refusing to receive a Russian one. An intimation was conveyed to the Ameer that if he should persist in his refusal to receive the mission, the Viceroy would have no other alternative than to regard Afghanistan as a state which had 'voluntarily isolated itself from the alliance and support of the British Government.' The Ameer arranged that the Vakeel of the Indian Government should visit Simla, carrying with him full explanations, and charged to lay before the Viceroy sundry grievances which were distressing Shere Ali. That functionary took back to Cabul certain minor concessions, but conveyed the message also that those concessions were contingent on the Ameer's acceptance of British officers about his frontiers, and that it would be of no avail to send an Envoy to the conference at Peshawur for which sanction was given, unless he were commissioned to agree to this condition as the fundamental basis of a treaty. Before the Vakeel quitted Simla he had to listen to a truculent address from Lord Lytton, in the course of which Shere Ali's position was genially likened to that of 'an earthen pipkin between two iron pots.' Before Sir Lewis Pelly and the Ameer's representative met at Peshawur in January 1877, Shere Ali had not unnaturally been perturbed by the permanent occupation of Quetta, on the southern verge of his dominions, as indicating, along with other military dispositions, an intended invasion. The Peshawur conference, which from the first had little promise, dragged on unsatisfactorily until terminated by the death of the Ameer's representative, whereupon Sir Lewis Pelly was recalled by Lord Lytton, notwithstanding the latter's cognisance that Shere Ali was despatching to Peshawur a fresh Envoy authorised to assent to all the British demands. The justification advanced by Lord Lytton for this procedure was the discovery purported to have been made by Sir Lewis Pelly that the Ameer was intriguing with General Kaufmann at Tashkend. Since Shere Ali was an independent monarch, it was no crime on his part to enter into negotiations with another power than Great Britain, although if the worried and distracted man did so the charge of folly may be laid to him, since the Russians were pretty certain to betray him after having made a cat's-paw of him, and since in applying to them he involved himself in the risk of hostile action on the part of the British. The wisdom of Lord Lytton's conduct is not apparent. The truculent policy of which he was the instrument was admittedly on the point of triumphing; and events curiously falsified his short-sighted anticipation of the unlikelihood, because of the Russo-Turkish war then impending, of any rapprochement between the Ameer and the Russian authorities in Central Asia. The Viceroy withdrew his Vakeel from Cabul, and in the recognition of the Ameer's attitude of 'isolation and scarcely veiled hostility' Lord Salisbury authorised Lord Lytton to protect the British frontier by such measures as circumstances should render expedient, 'without regard to the wishes of the Ameer or the interests of his dynasty.' Lord Lytton took no measures, expedient or otherwise, in the direction indicated by Lord Salisbury; the Ameer, as if he had been a petted boy consigned to the corner, was abandoned to his sullen 'isolation,' and the Russians adroitly used him to involve us in a war which lasted two years, cost us the lives of many valiant men, caused us to incur an expenditure of many millions, and left our relations with Afghanistan in all essential respects in the same condition as Lord Lytton found them when he reached India with the 'new policy' in his pocket.

If the Russians could execute as thoroughly as they can plan skilfully, there would be hardly any limit to their conquests. When England was mobilising her forces after the treaty of San Stefano, and ordering into the Mediterranean a division of sepoys drawn from the three presidencies of her Indian Empire, Russia for her part was concerting an important diversion in the direction of the north-western frontier of that great possession. But for the opportune conclusion of the treaty of Berlin, the question as to the ability of sepoy troops stiffened by British regiments to cope with the mixed levies of the Tzar might have been tried out on stricken fields between the Oxus and the Indus. When Gortschakoff returned from Berlin to St Petersburg with his version of 'Peace with Honour'--Bessarabia and Batoum thrown in--Kaufmann had to countermand the concentration of troops that had been in progress on the northern frontier of Afghanistan. But the Indian division was still much in evidence in the Mediterranean, its tents now gleaming on the brown slopes of Malta, now crowning the upland of Larnaca and nestling among the foliage of Kyrenea. Kaufmann astutely retorted on this demonstration by despatching, not indeed an expedition, but an embassy to Cabul; and when Stolietoff, the gallant defender of the Schipka Pass, rode into the Balla Hissar on August 11th, 1878, Shere Ali received him with every token of cordiality and regard.

No other course was now open to Her Majesty's Government than to insist on the reception at Cabul of a British mission. The gallant veteran officer Sir Neville Chamberlain, known to be held in regard by the Ameer, was named as Envoy, and an emissary was sent to Cabul in advance with information of the date fixed for the setting out of the mission. Shere Ali was greatly perplexed, and begged for more time. 'It is not proper,' he protested, 'to use pressure in this way; it will tend to a complete rupture.' But Sir Neville Chamberlain was satisfied that the Ameer was trifling with the Indian Government; and he had certain information that the Ameer, his Ministers, and the Afghan outpost officers, had stated plainly that, if necessary, the advance of the mission would be arrested by force. This was what in effect happened when on September 21st Major Cavagnari rode forward to the Afghan post in the Khyber Pass. The officer who courteously stopped him assured him that he had orders to oppose by force the progress of Sir Neville and his mission, so Cavagnari shook hands with the Afghan major and rode back to Peshawur.

The Viceroy sought permission to declare war immediately, notwithstanding his condition of unpreparedness; but the Home Government directed him instead to require in

CANDAHAR

temperate language an apology and the acceptance of a permanent mission, presenting at the same time the ultimatum that if a satisfactory reply should not be received on or before the 20th November hostilities would immediately commence. Meanwhile military preparations were actively pushed forward. The scheme of operations was as follows: three columns of invasion were to move simultaneously, one through the Khyber Pass to Dakka, another through the Kuram valley, south of the Khyber, with the Peiwar Pass as its objective, and a third from Quetta into the Pisheen valley, to march forward to Candahar after reinforcement by a division from Mooltan. To General Sir Sam Browne was assigned the command of the Khyber column, consisting of about 10,000 men, with thirty guns; to General Roberts the command of the Kuram valley column, of about 5,500 men, with twenty-four guns; and to General Biddulph the command of the Quetta force, numbering some 6000 men, with eighteen guns. When General Donald Stewart should bring up from Mooltan the division which was being concentrated there, he was to command the whole southern force moving on Candahar. The reserve division gathering at Hassan Abdul and commanded by General Maude, would support the Khyber force; another reserve division massing at Sukkur under General Primrose, would act in support of the Candahar force; and a contingent contributed by the Sikh Feudatory States and commanded by Colonel Watson, was to do duty on the Kurum line of communication. The Generals commanding columns were to act independently of each other, taking instructions direct from Army and Government headquarters.

No answer to the ultimatum was received from the Ameer, and on the morning of November 21st Sir Sam Browne crossed the Afghan frontier and moved up the Khyber on Ali Musjid with his third and fourth brigades and the guns. Overnight he had detached Macpherson's and Tytler's brigades with the commission to turn the Ali Musjid position by a circuitous march, the former charged to descend into the Khyber Pass in rear of the fortress, and block the escape of its garrison; the latter instructed to find, if possible, a position on the Rhotas heights on the proper left of the fortress from which a flank attack might be delivered. About noon Sir Sam reached the Shagai ridge and came under a brisk fire from the guns of Ali Musjid, to which his heavy cannon and Manderson's horse-battery replied with good results. The Afghan position, which was very strong, stretched right athwart the valley from an entrenched line on the right to the Rhotas summit on the extreme left. The artillery duel lasted about two hours, and then Sir Sam determined to advance, on the expectation that the turning brigades had reached their respective objectives. He himself moved forward on the right upland; on the opposite side of the Khyber stream Appleyard led the advance of his brigade against the Afghan right. No co-operation on the part of the turning brigades had made itself manifest up till dusk; the right brigade had been brought to a halt in face of a precipitous cliff crowned by the enemy, and it was wisely judged that to press the frontal attack further in the meantime would involve a useless loss of life. Sir Sam therefore halted, and sent word to Appleyard to stay for the night his further advance, merely holding the ridge which he had already carried. But before this order reached him Appleyard was sharply engaged with the enemy in their entrenched position, and in the fighting which occurred before the retirement was effected two officers were killed, a third wounded, and a good many casualties occurred among the rank and file of the native detachments gallantly assailing the Afghan entrenchments.

Early next morning offensive operations were about

to be resumed, when a young officer of the 9th Lancers brought intelligence that the Afghan garrison had fled under cover of night, whereupon the fort was promptly occupied. The turning brigades had been delayed by the difficult country encountered, but detachments from both had reached Kata Kustia in time to capture several hundred fugitives of the Ali Musjid garrison. The mass of it, however--its total strength was about 4000 men--effected a retreat by the Peshbolak track from the right of the entrenched position. Sir Sam Browne's advance to Dakka was made without molestation, and on 20th December he encamped on the plain of Jellalabad, where he remained throughout the winter, Maude's reserve division keeping open his communications through the Khyber Pass. The hill tribes, true to their nature, gave great annoyance by their continual raids, and several punitive expeditions were sent against them from time to time, but seldom with decisive results. The tribesmen for the most part carried off into the hills their moveable effects, and the destruction of their petty forts apparently gave them little concern. For the most part they maintained their irreconcilable attitude, hanging on the flanks of our detachments on their return march through the lateral passes to their camps, and inflicting irritating if not very severe losses. Occasionally they thought proper to make nominal submission with tongue in cheek, breaking out again when opportunity or temptation presented itself. Detailed description of those raids and counter-raids would be very tedious reading. It was when starting to co-operate in one of those necessary but tantalising expeditions that a number of troopers of the 10th Hussars were drowned in a treacherous ford of the Cabul river near Jellalabad.

General Roberts, to whom the conduct of operations in the Kuram district had been entrusted, crossed the frontier on November 21st, and marched up the valley with great expedition. The inhabitants evinced friendliness, bringing in live stock and provisions for sale. Reaching Habib Killa on the morning of the 28th, he received a report that the Afghan force which he knew to be opposed to him had abandoned its guns on the hither side of the Peiwar Kotul, and was retreating in confusion over that summit. Roberts promptly pushed forward in two columns. Building on the erroneous information that the enemy were in a hollow trying to withdraw their guns--in reality they were already in their entrenched position on the summit of the Kotul--he ordered Cobbe's (the left) column to turn the right of the supposed Afghan position, and debar the enemy from the Kotul, while the other column (Thelwall's) was ordered to attack in front, the object being to have the enemy between two fires. Cobbe's leading regiment near the village of Turrai found its advance blocked by precipices, and a withdrawal was ordered, the advantage having been attained of forcing the enemy to disclose the position which he was holding. Further reconnaissances proved that the Afghan line of defence extended along the crest of a lofty and broken mountainous range from the Spingawai summit on the left to the Peiwar Kotul on the right centre, the right itself resting on commanding elevations a mile further south. The position had a front in all of about four miles. It was afterwards ascertained to have been held by about 3500 regulars and a large number of tribal irregulars. General Roberts' force numbered about 3100 men.

His scheme of operations he explained to his commanding officers on the evening of December 1st. With the bulk of the force he himself was to make a circuitous night march by his right on the Spingawai Kotul, with the object of turning that position and taking the main Afghan position on the Peiwar Kotul in reverse; while Brigadier

ELEPHANT BATTERY

Cobbe, with whom were to remain the 8th (Queen's) and 5th Punjaub Infantry regiments, a cavalry regiment and six guns, was instructed to assail the enemy's centre when the result of the flank attack on his left should have made itself apparent.

The turning column, whose advance the General led in person, consisted of the 29th N. I. (leading), 5th Goorkhas, and a mountain battery, all under Colonel Gordon's command; followed by a wing of the 72d Highlanders, 2d Punjaub Infantry, and 23d Pioneers, with four guns on elephants, under Brigadier Thelwall. The arduous march began at ten P.M. Trending at first rearward to the Peiwar village, the course followed was then to the proper right, up the rugged and steep Spingawai ravine. In the darkness part of Thelwall's force lost its way, and disappeared from ken. Further on a couple of shots were fired by disaffected Pathans in the ranks of the 29th N. I. That regiment was promptly deprived of the lead, which was taken by the Goorkha regiment, and the column toiled on by a track described by General Roberts as 'nothing but a mass of stones, heaped into ridges and furrowed into deep hollows by the action of the water.' Day had not broken when the head of the column reached the foot of the steep ascent to the Spingawai Kotul. The Goorkhas and the 72d rushed forward on the first stockade. It was carried without a pause save to bayonet the defenders, and stockade after stockade was swept over in rapid and brilliant succession. In half-an-hour General Roberts was in full possession of the Spingawai defences, and the Afghan left flank was not only turned but driven in. Cobbe was ordered by signal to co-operate by pressing on his frontal attack; and Roberts himself hurried forward on his enterprise of rolling up the Afghan left and shaking its centre. But this proved no easy task. The Afghans made a good defence, and gave ground reluctantly. They made a resolute stand on the further side of a narrow deep-cut ravine, to dislodge them from which effort after effort was ineffectually made. The General then determined to desist from pressing this line of attack, and to make a second turning movement by which he hoped to reach the rear of the Afghan centre. He led the 72d wing, three native regiments, and ten guns, in a direction which should enable him to threaten the line of the Afghan retreat. Brigadier Cobbe since morning had been steadily although slowly climbing toward the front of the Peiwar Kotul position. After an artillery duel which lasted for three hours the Afghan fire was partially quelled; Cobbe's infantry pushed on and up from ridge to ridge, and at length they reached a crest within 800 yards of the guns on the Kotul, whence their rifle fire compelled the Afghan gunners to abandon their batteries. Meanwhile Roberts' second turning movement was developing, and the defenders of the Kotul placed between two fires and their line of retreat compromised, began to waver. Brigadier Cobbe had been wounded, but Colonel Drew led forward his gallant youngsters of the 8th, and after toilsome climbing they entered the Afghan position, which its defenders had just abandoned, leaving many dead, eighteen guns, and a vast accumulation of stores and ammunition. Colonel H. Gough pursued with his cavalry, and possessed himself of several more guns which the Afghans had relinquished in their precipitate flight. The decisive success of the Peiwar Kotul combat had not cost heavily; the British losses were twenty-one killed and seventy-two wounded.

His sick and wounded sent back to Fort Kuram, General Roberts advanced to Ali Khel, and thence made a reconnaissance forward to the Shutargurdan Pass, whose summit is distant from Cabul little more than fifty miles. Its height is great--upwards of 11,200 feet--but it was regarded as not presenting serious obstacles to the advance by this route of a force from the Kuram valley moving on Cabul. A misfortune befell the baggage guard on one of the marches in the trans-Peiwar region when Captains Goad and Powell lost their lives in a tribal onslaught. The somewhat chequered experiences of General Roberts in the Khost valley need not be told in detail. After some fighting and more marching he withdrew from that turbulent region altogether, abjuring its pestilent tribesmen and all their works. The Kuram force wintered in excellent health spite of the rigorous climate, and toward the end of March 1879 its forward concentration about Ali Kheyl was ordered, which was virtually accomplished before the snow had melted from the passes in the later weeks of April. Adequate transport had been got together and supplies accumulated; Colonel Watson's contingent was occupying the posts along the valley; and General Roberts was in full readiness promptly to obey the orders to advance which he had been led to expect, and on which his brother-general Sir Sam Browne had already acted to some extent.

The march on Candahar of the two divisions under the command of General Stewart had the character, for the most part, of a military promenade. The tramp across the deserts of Northern Beloochistan was arduous; the Bolan, the Gwaga, and the Kojuk passes had to be surmounted, and the distances which both Biddulph and Stewart had to traverse were immensely in excess of those covered by either of the forces operating from the north-western frontier line. But uneventful marches, however long and toilsome, do not call for detailed description. Stewart rode into Candahar on January 8th, 1879, and the troops as they arrived encamped on the adjacent plain. The Governor and most of his officials, together with the Afghan cavalry, had fled toward Herat; the Deputy-Governor remained to hand over the city to General Stewart. For commissariat reasons one division under Stewart presently moved by the Cabul road on Khelat-i-Ghilzai, which was found empty, the Afghan garrison having evacuated it. Simultaneously with Stewart's departure from Candahar Biddulph marched out a column westward toward the Helmund, remaining in that region until the third week in February. On its return march to Candahar the rear-guard had a sharp skirmish at Khushk-i-Nakhud with Alizai tribesmen, of whom 163 were left dead on the field. Soon after the return of Stewart and Biddulph to Candahar, orders arrived that the former should retain in Candahar, Quetta, and Pishin a strong division of all arms, sending back to India the remainder of his command under Biddulph--the march to be made by the previously unexplored Thal-Chotiali route to the eastward of the Pisheen valley.

Before Sir Sam Browne moved forward from Jellalabad to Gundamuk he had been able to report to the Viceroy the death of Shere Ali. That unfortunate man had seen with despair the departure on December 10th of the last Russian from Cabul--sure token that he need hope for nothing from Kaufmann or the Tzar. His chiefs unanimous that further resistance by him was hopeless, he released his son Yakoub Khan from his long harsh imprisonment, constituted him Regent, and then followed the Russian mission in the direction of Tashkend. Kaufmann would not so much as allow him to cross the frontier, and after a painful illness Shere Ali died on February 21st, 1879, near Balkh in northern Afghanistan. He was a man who deserved a better fate than that which befell him. His aspiration was to maintain the independence of the kingdom which he ruled with justice if also with masterfulness, and he could not brook the degradation of subjection. But, unfortunately for him, he was the 'earthen pipkin' which the 'iron pot' found inconvenient. There had been plenty of man-

BRITISH FIRING

hood originally in his son and successor Yakoub Khan, but much of that attribute had withered in him during the long cruel imprisonment to which he had been subjected by his father. Shere Ali's death made him nominal master of Afghanistan, but the vigour of his youth-time no longer characterised him. He reigned but did not rule, and how precarious was his position was evidenced by the defection of many leading chiefs who came into the English camps and were ready to make terms.

After the flight of Shere Ali some correspondence had passed between Yakoub Khan and Major Cavagnari, but the former had not expressed any willingness for the re-establishment of friendly relations. In February of his own accord he made overtures for a reconciliation, and soon after intimated the death of his father and his own accession to the Afghan throne. Major Cavagnari, acting on the Viceroy's authorisation, wrote to the new sovereign stating the terms on which the Anglo-Indian Government was prepared to engage in negotiations for peace. Yakoub temporised for some time, but influenced by the growing defection of the Sirdars from his cause, as well as by the forward movements of the forces commanded by Browne and Roberts, he intimated his intention of visiting Gundamuk in order to discuss matters in personal conference with Major Cavagnari. A fortnight later he was on his way down the passes.

Instructions had been given by the Viceroy that Yakoub Khan should be received in the British camp with all honour and distinction. When his approach was announced on May 8th, Cavagnari and a number of British officers rode out to meet him; when he reached the camp, a royal salute greeted him, a guard of honour presented arms, and Sir Sam Browne and his staff gave him a ceremonious welcome. Cavagnari had full powers to represent his Government in the pending negotiations, as to the terms of which he had received from the Viceroy detailed instructions. The Ameer and his General-in-Chief, Daoud Shah, came to the conference attired in Russian uniforms. The negotiations were tedious, for the Ameer, his Minister, and his General made difficulties with a somewhat elaborate stupidity, but Cavagnari as a diplomatist possessed the gift of being at once patient and firm; and at length on May 26th the treaty of peace was signed, and formally ratified by the Viceroy four days later. By the treaty of Gundamuk Afghanistan was deprived for the time of its traditional character of a 'buffer state,' and its Ameer became virtually a feudatory of the British Crown. He was no longer an independent prince; although his titular rank and a nominal sovereignty remained to him, his position under its articles was to be analogous to that of the mediatised princes of the German Empire. The treaty vested in the British Government the control of the external relations of Afghanistan. The Ameer consented to the residence of British Agents within his dominions, guaranteeing their safety and honourable treatment, while the British Government undertook that its representatives should not interfere with the internal administration of the country. The districts of Pisheen, Kuram, and Sibi were ceded to the British Government along with the permanent control of the Khyber and Michnai passes, and of the mountain tribes inhabiting the vicinity of those passes; all other Afghan territory in British occupation was to be restored. The obligations to which the treaty committed the British Government were that it should support the Ameer against foreign aggression with arms, money, or troops at its discretion, and that it should pay to him and his successor an annual subsidy of £60,000. Commercial relations between India and Afghanistan were to be protected and encouraged; a telegraph line between Cabul and the

Kuram was forthwith to be constructed; and the Ameer was to proclaim an amnesty relieving all and sundry of his subjects from punishment for services rendered to the British during the war.

That the treaty of Gundamuk involved our Indian Empire in serious responsibilities is obvious, and those responsibilities were the more serious that they were vague and indefinite, yet none the less binding on this account. It is probable that its provisions, if they had remained in force, would have been found in the long run injurious to the interests of British India. For that realm Afghanistan has the value that its ruggedness presents exceptional obstacles to the march through it of hostile armies having the Indian frontier for their objective, and this further and yet more important value that the Afghans by nature are frank and impartial Ishmaelites, their hands against all foreigners alike, no matter of what nationality. If this character be impaired, what virtue the Afghan has in our eyes is lost. In his implacable passion for independence, in his fierce intolerance of the Feringhee intruder, he fulfils in relation to our Indian frontier a kindred office to that served by abattis, cheveux de frise, and wire entanglements in front of a military position. The short-lived treaty, for which the sanguine Mr Stanhope claimed that it had gained for England 'a friendly, an independent, and a strong Afghanistan,' may now be chiefly remembered because of the circumstance that it gave effect for the moment to Lord Beaconsfield's 'scientific frontier.'

The withdrawal of the two northern forces to positions within the new frontier began immediately on the ratification of the treaty of Gundamuk, the evacuation of Candahar being postponed for sanitary reasons until autumn. The march of Sir Sam Browne's force from the breezy upland of Gundamuk down the passes to Peshawur, made as it was in the fierce heat of midsummer through a region of bad name for insalubrity, and pervaded also by virulent cholera, was a ghastly journey. That melancholy pilgrimage, every halting-place in whose course was marked by graves, and from which the living emerged 'gaunt and haggard, marching with a listless air, their clothing stiff with dried perspiration, their faces thick with a mud of dust and sweat through which their red bloodshot eyes looked forth, many suffering from heat prostration,' dwells in the memory of British India as the 'death march,' and its horrors have been recounted in vivid and pathetic words by Surgeon-Major Evatt, one of the few medical officers whom, participating in it, it did not kill.

CHAPTER 2

The Opening of the
Second Campaign

There were many who mistrusted the stability of the treaty of Gundamuk. Perhaps in his heart Sir Louis Cavagnari may have had his misgivings, for he was gifted with shrewd insight, and no man knew the Afghan nature better; but outwardly, in his quiet, resolute manner, he professed the fullest confidence. Cavagnari was a remarkable man. Italian and Irish blood commingled in his veins. Both strains carry the attributes of vivacity and restlessness, but Cavagnari to the superficial observer appeared as phlegmatic as he was habitually taciturn. This sententious imperturbability was only on the surface; whether it was a natural characteristic or an acquired manner is not easy to decide. Below the surface of measured reticent composure there lay a temperament of ardent enthusiasm, and not less ardent ambition. In subtlety he was a match for the wiliest Oriental, whom face to face he dominated with a placid dauntless masterfulness that was all his own. The wild hill tribes among whom he went about escortless, carrying his life continually in his hand, recognised the complex strength of his personal sway, and feared at once and loved the quiet, firm man, the flash of whose eye was sometimes ominous, but who could cow the fiercest hillman without losing a tittle of his cool composure.

Cavagnari had negotiated the treaty of Gundamuk, the real importance of which consisted in the Afghan acceptance of a British Resident at Cabul. The honour, the duty, and the danger naturally fell to him of being the first occupant of a post created mainly by his own mingled tact and strength. Many of his friends regarded him in the light of the leader of a forlorn hope, and probably Cavagnari recognised with perfect clearness the risks which encompassed his embassy; but apart from mayhap a little added gravity in his leave-takings when he quitted Simla, he gave no sign. It was not a very imposing mission at whose head he rode into the Balla Hissar of Cabul on July 24th, 1879. His companions were his secretary, Mr William Jenkins, a young Scotsman of the Punjaub Civil Service, Dr Ambrose Kelly, the medical officer of the embassy, and the gallant, stalwart young Lieutenant W. R. P. Hamilton, V.C., commanding the modest escort of seventy-five soldiers of the Guides. It was held that an escort so scanty was sufficient, since the Ameer had pledged himself personally for the safety and protection of the mission. The Envoy was received with high honour, and conducted to the roomy quarters in the Balla Hissar which had been prepared as the Residency, within easy distance of the Ameer's palace. Unquestionably the mission was welcome neither to the Afghan ruler nor to the people, but Cavagnari, writing to the Viceroy, made the best of things. The arrival at the adjacent Sherpur cantonments of the Herat regiments in the beginning of August was extremely unfortunate for the mission. Those troops had been inspired by their commander Ayoub Khan with intense hatred to the English, and they marched through the Cabul streets shouting objurgations against the British Envoy, and picking quarrels with the soldiers of his escort. A pensioned sepoy who had learned that the Afghan troops had been ordered to abuse the Eltchi, warned Cavagnari of the danger signals. Cavagnari's calm remark was, 'Dogs that bark don't bite.' The old soldier earnestly urged, 'But these

Afghan–Sherpur Assault

dogs do bite, and there is danger.' 'Well,' said Cavagnari, 'they can only kill the handful of us here, and our death will be avenged.' The days passed, and it seemed that Cavagnari's diagnosis of the situation was the accurate one. The last words of his last message to the Viceroy, despatched on September 2d, were 'All well.' The writer of those words was a dead man, and his mission had perished with him, almost as soon as the cheerful message borne along the telegraph wires reached its destination.

In the morning of September 3d some Afghan regiments paraded without arms in the Balla Hissar to receive their pay. An instalment was paid, but the soldiers clamoured for arrears due. The demand was refused, a riot began, and the shout rose that the British Eltchi might prove a free-handed paymaster. There was a rush toward the Residency, and while some of the Afghan soldiers resorted to stone-throwing, others ran for arms to their quarters, and looted the Arsenal in the upper Balla Hissar. The Residency gates had been closed on the first alarm, and fire was promptly opened on the rabble. The place was never intended for defence, commanded as it was at close range from the higher level of the Arsenal, whence a heavy continuous fire was from the first poured down. The mob of the city in their thousands hurried to co-operate with the mutinied soldiers and share in the spoils of the sack, so that the Residency was soon besieged. As soon as the outbreak manifested itself Cavagnari had sent a message to the Ameer, and the communication admittedly reached the latter's hands. He had more than 2000 troops in the Balla Hissar, still at least nominally loyal; he had guaranteed the protection of the mission, and it behoved him to do what in him lay to fulfil his pledge. But the Ameer sat supine in his palace, doing no more than send his General-in-Chief Daoud Shah to remonstrate with the insurgents. Daoud Shah went on the errand, but it is questionable whether he showed any energy, or indeed desired that the besiegers should desist. It was claimed by and for him that he was maltreated and indeed wounded by the mob, and it appears that he did ride into the throng and was forcibly dismounted. He might perhaps have exerted himself with greater determination if he had received more specific orders from his master the Ameer. That feeble or treacherous prince never stirred. To the frequent urgent messages sent him by Lieutenant Hamilton, he replied vaguely: 'As God wills; I am making preparations.' Meanwhile the little garrison maintained with gallant staunchness hour after hour the all but hopeless defence.' While the fighting was going on,' reported the pensioner who had previously warned Cavagnari, 'I myself saw the four European officers charge out at the head of some twenty-five of the garrison; they drove away a party holding some broken ground. When chased, the Afghan soldiers ran like sheep before a wolf. Later, another sally was made by a detachment, with but three officers at their head. Cavagnari was not with them this time. A third sally was made with only two officers leading, Hamilton and Jenkins; and the last of the sallies was made by a Sikh Jemadar bravely leading. No more sallies were made after this.' About noon the gates were forced, and the Residency building was fired; but the defenders long maintained their position on the roof and in a detached building. At length the fire did its work, the walls and roof fell in, and soon the fell deed was consummated by the slaughter of the last survivors of the ill-fated garrison. Hamilton was said to have died sword in hand in a final desperate charge. Tidings of the massacre were carried with great speed to Massy's outposts in the Kuram valley. The news reached Simla by telegraph early on the morning of the 5th. The authorities there rallied from the shock with fine purposeful promptitude, and within a few hours a telegram was on its way to General Massy's headquarters at Ali Khel instructing him to occupy the crest of the Shutargurdan Pass with two infantry regiments and a mountain battery, which force was to entrench itself there and await orders.

The policy of which Lord Lytton was the figurehead had come down with a bloody crash, and the 'masterly inactivity' of wise John Lawrence stood vindicated in the eyes of Europe and of Asia. But if his policy had gone to water, the Viceroy, although he was soon to default from the constancy of his purpose, saw for the present clear before him the duty that now in its stead lay upon him of inflicting summary punishment on a people who had ruthlessly violated the sacred immunity from harm that shields alike among civilised and barbarous communities the person and suite of an ambassador accepted under the provisions of a deliberate treaty. Burnes and Macnaghten had met their fate because they had gone to Cabul the supporters of a detested intruder and the unwelcome representatives of a hated power. But Cavagnari had been slaughtered notwithstanding that he dwelt in the Balla Hissar Residency in virtue of a solemn treaty between the Empress of India and the Ameer of Afghanistan, notwithstanding that the latter had guaranteed him safety and protection, notwithstanding that Britain and Afghanistan had ratified a pledge of mutual friendship and reciprocal good offices. Lord Lytton recognised, at least for the moment, that no consideration of present expediency or of ulterior policy could intervene to deter him from the urgent imperative duty which now suddenly confronted him. The task, it was true, was beset with difficulties and dangers. The forces on the northwestern frontier had been reduced to a peace footing, and the transport for economical reasons had been severely cut down. The bitter Afghan winter season was approaching, during which military operations could be conducted only under extremely arduous conditions, and when the line of communications would be liable to serious interruptions, The available troops for a prompt offensive did not amount to more than 6500 men all told, and it was apparent that many circumstances might postpone their reinforcement.

When men are in earnest, difficulties and dangers are recognised only to be coped with and overcome. When the Simla council of war broke up on the afternoon of September 5th the plan of campaign had been settled, and the leader of the enterprise had been chosen. Sir Frederick Roberts was already deservedly esteemed one of the most brilliant soldiers of the British army. He had fought with distinction all through the Great Mutiny, earning the Victoria Cross and rapid promotion; he had served in the Abyssinian campaign of 1868, and been chosen by Napier to carry home his final despatches; and he had worthily shared in the toil, fighting, and honours of the Umbeyla and Looshai expeditions. In his command of the Kuram field force during the winter of 1878-9 he had proved himself a skilful, resolute, and vigorous leader. The officers and men who served under him believed in him enthusiastically, and, what with soldiers is the convincing assurance of whole-souled confidence, they had bestowed on him an affectionate nickname--they knew him among themselves as 'little Bobs.' His administrative capacity he had proved in the post of Quartermaster-General in India. Ripe in experience of war, Roberts at the age of forty-seven was in the full vigour of manhood, alert in mind, and of tough and enduring physique. He was a very junior Major-General, but even among his seniors the conviction was general that Lord Lytton the Viceroy, and Sir F. Haines the Commander-in-Chief, acted wisely in entrusting to him the most active command in the impending campaign.

Our retention of the Kuram valley was to prove very useful in the emergency which had suddenly occurred. Its occupation enabled Massy to seize and hold the Shutargurdan, and the force in the valley was to constitute the nucleus of the little army of invasion and retribution to the command of which Sir Frederick Roberts was appointed. The apex at the Shutargurdan of the salient angle into Afghanistan which our possession of the Kuram valley furnished was within little more than fifty miles of Cabul, whereas the distance of that city from Lundi Kotul, our advanced position at the head of the Khyber Pass, was about 140 miles, and the route exceptionally difficult. Roberts' column of invasion was to consist of a cavalry brigade commanded by Brigadier-General Dunham-Massy, and of two infantry brigades, the first commanded by Brigadier-General Macpherson, the second by Brigadier-General Baker, three batteries of artillery, a company of sappers and miners, and two Gatling guns. The Kuram valley between the Shutargurdan and the base was to be garrisoned adequately by a force about 4000 strong, in protection of Roberts' communications by that line until snow should close it, by which time it was anticipated that communication by the Khyber-Jellalabad-Gundamuk line would be opened up, for gaining and maintaining which a force of about 6600 men was to be detailed under the command of Major-General Bright, which was to furnish a movable column to establish communications onward to Cabul. A strong reserve force was to be gathered between Peshawur and Rawal Pindi under the command of Major-General Ross, to move forward as occasion might require, in the south-west Sir Donald Stewart was to recall to Candahar his troops, which, having begun their march toward India, were now mainly echeloned along the route to Quetta, when that General would have about 9000 men at his disposition to dominate the Candahar province, reoccupy Khelat-i-Ghilzai, and threaten Ghuznee, his communications with the Indus being kept open by a brigade of Bombay troops commanded by Brigadier-General Phayre.

Sir Frederick Roberts left Simla on ET September along with Colonel Charles Macgregor, C.B., the brilliant and daring soldier whom he had chosen as chief of staff, and travelling night and day they reached Ali Khel on the 12th. The transport and supply difficulty had to be promptly met, and this was effected only by making a clean sweep of all the resources of the Peshawur district, greatly but unavoidably to the hindrance of the advance of the Khyber column, and by procuring carriage and supplies from the friendly tribes of the Kuram. Notwithstanding the most strenuous exertions it was not until the 1st October that Roberts' little army, having crossed the Shutargurdan by detachments, was rendezvoused at and about the village of Kushi in the Logur plain, within forty-eight miles of Cabul. Some sharp skirmishes had been fought as the troops traversed the rugged ground between Ali Khel and the Shutargurdan, but the losses were trivial, although the General himself had a narrow escape. A couple of regiments and four guns under the command of Colonel Money were left in an entrenched camp to hold the Shutargurdan.

The massacre of the British mission had no sooner been perpetrated than Yakoub Khan found himself in a very bad way. The Cabul Sirdars sided with the disaffected soldiery, and urged the Ameer to raise his banner for a jehad or religious war, a measure for which he had no nerve. Nor had he the nerve to remain in Cabul until Roberts should camp under the Balla Hissar and demand of him an account of the stewardship he had undertaken on behalf of the ill-fated Cavagnari. What reasons actuated the anxious and bewildered man cannot precisely be known; whether he was simply solicitous for his own wretched skin, whether he acted from a wish to save Cabul from destruction, or whether he hoped that his entreaties for delay might stay the British advance until the tribesmen should gather to bar the road to the capital. He resolved to fly from Cabul, and commit himself to the protection of General Roberts and his army. The day before General Roberts arrived at Kushi the Ameer presented himself in Baker's camp, accompanied by his eldest son and some of his Sirdars, among whom was Daoud Shah the Commander-in-Chief of his army. Sir Frederick on his arrival at Kushi paid a formal visit to the Ameer, which the latter returned the same afternoon and took occasion to plead that the General should delay his advance. The reply was that not even for a single day would Sir Frederick defer his march on Cabul. The Ameer remained in camp, his personal safety carefully protected, but under a species of honourable surveillance, until it should be ascertained judicially whether or not he was implicated in the massacre of the mission.

Yakoub had intimated his intention of presenting himself in the British camp some days in advance of his arrival, and as telegraphic communication with headquarters was open, his acceptance in the character of an honoured guest was presumably in accordance with instructions from Simla. The man who had made himself personally responsible for the safety of Cavagnari's mission was a strange guest with an army whose avowed errand was to exact retribution for the crime of its destruction. It might seem not unreasonable to expect that, as an indispensable preliminary to his entertainment, he should have at least afforded some prima facie evidence that he had been zealous to avert the fate which had befallen the mission, and stern in the punishment of an atrocity which touched him so nearly. But instead, he was taken on trust so fully that Afghans resisting

41

the British advance were not so much regarded as enemies resisting an invasion and as constructive vindicators of the massacre, as they were held traitors to their sovereign harbouring in the British camp.

On the morning of October 2d the whole force marched from Kushi toward Cabul, temporarily cutting loose from communication with the Shutargurdan, to avoid diminishing the strength of the column by leaving detachments to keep the road open. All told, Roberts' army was the reverse of a mighty host. Its strength was little greater than that of a Prussian brigade on a war footing. Its fate was in its own hands, for befall it what might it could hope for no timely reinforcement. It was a mere detachment marching against a nation of fighting men plentifully supplied with artillery, no longer shooting laboriously with jezails, but carrying arms of precision equal or little inferior to those in the hands of our own soldiery. But the men, Europeans and Easterns, hillmen of Scotland and hillmen of Nepaul, plainmen of Hampshire and plainmen of the Punjaub, strode along buoyant with confidence and with health, believing in their leader, in their discipline, in themselves. Of varied race, no soldier who followed Roberts but came of fighting stock; ever blithely rejoicing in the combat, one and all burned for the strife now before them with more than wonted ardour, because of the opportunity it promised to exact vengeance for a deed of foul treachery.

The soldiers had not long to wait for the first fight of the campaign. On the afternoon of the 5th Baker's brigade, with most of the cavalry and artillery, and with the 92d Highlanders belonging to Macpherson's brigade, camped on the plain to the south of the village of Charasiah, Macpherson remaining one march in rear to escort the convoy of ammunition and stores. North of Charasiah rises a semicircular curtain of hills ascending in three successive tiers, the

The 92nd Highlanders

most distant and loftiest range closing in the horizon and shutting out the view of Cabul, distant only about eleven miles. The leftward projection of the curtain, as one looks northward, comes down into the plain almost as far as and somewhat to the left of Charasiah, dividing the valley of Charasiah from the outer plain of Chardeh. To the right front of Charasiah, distant from it about three miles, the range is cleft by the rugged and narrow Sung-i-Nawishta Pass, through which run the Logur river and the direct road to Cabul by Beni Hissar. Information had been received that the Afghans were determined on a resolute attempt to prevent the British force from reaching Cabul, and the position beyond Charasiah seemed so tempting that it was regarded as surprising that cavalry reconnaissances sent forward on three distinct roads detected no evidences of any large hostile gathering.

But next morning 'showed another sight.' At dawn on the 6th General Roberts, anxious to secure the Sung-i-Nawishta Pass and to render the track through it passable for guns, sent forward his pioneer battalion with a wing of the 92d and two mountain guns. That detachment had gone out no great distance when the spectacle before it gave it pause. From the Sung-i-Nawishta defile, both sides of which were held, the semicircular sweep of the hill-crests was crowned by an Afghan host in great strength and regular formation. According to subsequent information no fewer than thirteen regiments of the Afghan regular army took part in the combat, as well as large contingents of irregular fighting men from Cabul and the adjoining villages, while the British camp was threatened from the heights on either side by formidable bodies of tribesmen, to thwart whose obviously intended attack on it a considerable force had to be retained. The dispositions of the Afghan commander Nek Mahomed Khan were made with some tactical skill. The Sung-i-Nawishta Pass itself, the heights on either side, and a low detached eminence further forward, were strongly held by Afghan infantry; in the mouth of the pass were four Armstrong guns, and on the flanking height twelve mountain guns were in position. The projecting spur toward Charasiah which was the extreme right of the Afghan position, was held in force, whence an effective fire would bear on the left flank of a force advancing to a direct attack on the pass. But Roberts was not the man to play into the hands of the Afghan tactician. He humoured his conception so far as to send forward on his right toward the pass, a small detachment of all arms under Major White of the 92d, with instructions to maintain a threatening attitude in that direction, and to seize the opportunity to co-operate with the flanking movement entrusted to General Baker as soon as its development should have shaken the constancy of the enemy. To Baker with about 2000 infantry and four guns, was assigned the task of attacking the Afghan right on the projecting spur and ridge, forcing back and dispersing that flank; and then, having reached the right of the Afghan main position on the farthest and loftiest range, he was to wheel to his right and sweep its defenders from the chain of summits.

Baker moved out toward his left front against the eminences held by the Afghan right wing, which Nek Mahomed, having discerned the character of Roberts' tactics, was now reinforcing with great activity. The 72d Highlanders led the attack, supported vigorously by the 5th Goorkhas and the 5th Punjaub Infantry. The resistance of the Afghans was stubborn, especially opposite our extreme left, whence from behind their sungahs on a steep hill they poured a heavy fire on the assailants. A yet heavier fire came from a detached knoll on Baker's right, which the artillery fire gradually beat down. The Afghans continued to hold the advanced ridge constituting their first position until two o'clock, when a direct attack, accompanied by a double flanking fire, compelled their withdrawal. They, however, fell back only to an intermediate loftier position about 700 yards in rear of the ridge from which they had been driven. Approached by successive rushes under cover-of artillery fire, they were then attacked vigorously and fell back in confusion. No rally was permitted them, and by three o'clock the whole Afghan right was shattered and in full flight along the edge of the Chardeh valley. Baker unfortunately had no cavalry, else the fugitives would have suffered severely. But the rout of the Afghan right had decided the fortune of the day. Its defenders were already dribbling away from the main position when Baker, wheeling to his right, marched along the lofty crest, rolling up and sweeping away the Afghan defence as he moved toward the Sung-i-Nawishta gorge. That defile had already been entered by the cavalry of White's detachment, supported by some infantry. While Baker had been turning the Afghan right, White and his little force had been distinguishing themselves not a little. After an artillery preparation the detached hill had been won as the result of a hand-to-hand struggle. Later had fallen into the hands of White's people all the Afghan guns, and the heights to the immediate right and left of the gorge had been carried, the defenders driven away, and the pass opened up. But the progress through it of the cavalry was arrested by a strongly garrisoned fort completely commanding the road. On this fort Baker directed his artillery fire, at the same time sending down two infantry regiments to clear away the remnants of the Afghan army still lingering in the pass. This accomplished, the fighting ceased. It had been a satisfactory day. Less than half of Roberts' force had been engaged, and this mere brigade had routed the army of Cabul and captured the whole of the artillery it had brought into the field. The Afghan loss was estimated at about 300 killed. The British loss was twenty killed and sixty-seven wounded. On the night of the combat part of Baker's troops bivouacked beyond the Sung-i-Nawishta, and on the following day the whole division passed the defile and camped at Beni Hissar, within sight of the Balla Hissar and the lofty ridge overhanging Cabul.

On the afternoon of the 7th a violent explosion was heard in the Beni Hissar camp from the direction of the Sherpur cantonment north of Cabul, near the site of the British cantonments of 1839-41. Next morning information came in that the Sherpur magazine had been blown up, and that the cantonment had been abandoned by the Afghan regiments which had garrisoned that vast unfinished structure. General Massy led out part of his brigade on a reconnaissance, and took possession of the deserted Sherpur cantonment, and of the seventy-five pieces of ordnance parked within the walls. Massy had observed from the Siah Sung heights that the Asmai heights, overhanging the Cabul suburb of Deh Afghan, were held by a large body of Afghan soldiery, a force, it was afterwards learned, composed of the remnants of the regiments defeated at Charasiah, three fresh regiments from the Kohistan, and the rabble of the city and adjacent villages, having a total strength of nearly 3000 men, with twelve guns, under the leadership of Mahomed Jan, who later was to figure prominently as the ablest of our Afghan enemies. Massy heliographed his information to General Roberts, who sent Baker with a force to drive the enemy from the heights; and Massy was instructed to pass through a gap in the ridge and gain the Chardeh valley, where he might find opportunity to intercept the Afghan retreat toward the west. Massy pierced the ridge at the village of Aushar, and disposed his troops on the roads crossing the Chardeh valley. Meanwhile Baker found the ascent of the Sher Derwaza heights so steep that the afternoon was far spent before his guns came into action, and it was still later before part of his infantry effected their descent into the Chardeh valley. Reinforcements necessary to enable him to act did not reach him until dusk, when it would have been folly to commit himself to an attack. A night patrol ascertained that the Afghans had evacuated the position under cover of darkness, leaving behind their guns and camp equipage. On the 9th the divisional camp moved forward to the Siah Sung heights, a mile eastward from the Balla Hissar, and there it was joined by Baker, and by Massy, who on his way to camp led his wearied troopers through the city of Cabul without mishap or insult. The Goorkha regiment was detached to hold the ridge commanding the Balla Hissar, and a cavalry regiment was quartered in the Sherpur cantonment to protect it from the ravages of the villagers.

A melancholy interest attaches to the visit paid by Sir Frederick Roberts to the Balla Hissar on the 11th. Through the dirt and squalor of the lower portion he ascended the narrow lane leading to the ruin which a few weeks earlier had been the British Residency. The commander of the avenging army looked with sorrowful eyes on the scene of heroism and slaughter, on the smoke-blackened walls, the blood splashes on the whitewashed walls, the still smouldering debris, the half-burned skulls and bones in the blood-dabbled chamber where apparently the final struggle had been fought out. He stood in the great breach in the quarters of the Guides where the gate had been blown in after the last of the sorties made by the gallant Hamilton, and lingered in the tattered wreck of poor Cavagnari's drawing-room, its walls dinted with bullet-pits, its floor and walls brutally de-

AFGHAN TRIBESMEN

filed. Next day he made a formal entry into the Balla Hissar, his road lined with his staunch troops, a royal salute greeting the banner of Britain as it rose on the tall flagstaff above the gateway. He held a Durbar in the 'Audience Chamber' in the garden of the Ameer's palace; in front and in flank of him the pushing throng of obsequious Sirdars of Cabul arrayed in all the colours of the rainbow; behind them, standing immobile at attention, the guard of British infantry with fixed bayonets which the soldiers longed to use. The General read the mild proclamation announcing the disarmament of the Cabulese and the punishment of fine which was laid upon the city, but which never was exacted. And then he summarily dismissed the Sirdars, three only, the Mustaphi, Yahuja Khan the Ameer's father-in-law, and Zakariah Khan his brother, being desired to remain. Their smug complacency was suddenly changed into dismay when they were abruptly told that they were prisoners.

Another ceremonial progress the General had to perform. On the 13th he marched through the streets of Cabul at the head of his little army, the bazaars and dead walls echoing to the music of the bands and the wild scream of the bagpipes. In the Afghan quarter no salaams greeted the conquering Feringhees, and scowling faces frowned on the spectacle from windows and side-streets. Three days later occurred an event which might have been a great catastrophe. Captain Shafto of the ordnance was conducting an examination into the contents of the arsenal in the upper Balla Hissar, and had already discovered millions of cartridges, and about 150,000 lbs. of gunpowder. Daoud Shah, however, expressed his belief that at least a million pounds were in store. Captain Shafto, a very cautious man, was pursuing his researches; the Goorkhas were quartered in the upper Balla Hissar near the magazine shed, and the 67th occupied the Ameer's garden lower down. On the

16th a dull report was heard in the Siah Sung camp, followed immediately by the rising above the Balla Hissar of a huge column of grey smoke, which as it drifted away disclosed flashes of flame and sudden jets of smoke telling of repeated gunpowder explosions. The 67th, powdered with dust, escaped all but scathless; but the Goorkha regiment had been heavily smitten. Twelve poor fellows were killed, and seven wounded; among the former were five principal Goorkha officers.

The Balla Hissar was promptly evacuated. Occasional explosions occurred for several days, the heaviest of those on the afternoon of the 16th, which threw on the city a great shower of stones, beams, and bullets. By a jet of stones blown out through the Balla Hissar gate four Afghans were killed, and two sowars and an Afghan badly hurt. Captain Shafto's body and the remains of the Goorkhas were found later, and buried; and the determination was formed to have no more to do with the Balla Hissar, but to occupy the Sherpur cantonment. Meanwhile General Hugh Gough was despatched with a small force of all arms to escort to Cabul Money's gallant garrison of the Shutargurdan, and to close for the winter the line of communication via the Kuram valley. Colonel Money had undergone with fine soldierly spirit and action not a few turbulent experiences since Roberts had left him and his Sikhs on the lofty crest of the Shutargurdan. The truculent Ghilzais gave him no peace; his method of dealing with them was for the most part with the bayonet point. The last attempt on him was made by a horde of Ghilzais some 17,000 strong, who completely invested his camp, and after the civility of requesting him to surrender, a compliment which he answered by bullets, made a close and determined attack on his position. This was on the 18th October; on the following day Gough heliographed his arrival at Kushi, whereupon Money took the offensive with vigour and scattered to the winds his Ghilzai assailants. On 30th October the Shutargurdan position was evacuated, and on the 3d November the Cabul force received the welcome accession of headquarters and two squadrons 9th Lancers, Money's 3d Sikhs, and four mountain guns.

CHAPTER 3

The Lull Before the Storm

Sir Frederick Roberts had been hurried forward on Cabul charged with the duty of avenging the perpetration of a foul and treacherous crime, 'which had brought indelible disgrace upon the Afghan nation.' The scriptural injunction to turn the other cheek to the smiter has not yet become a canon of international law or practice; and the anti-climax to an expedition engaged in with so stern a purpose, of a nominal disarmament and a petty fine never exacted, is self-evident. Our nation is given to walk in the path of precedent; and in this juncture the authorities had to their hand the most apposite of precedents. Pollock, by destroying the Char bazaar in which had been exposed the mangled remains of Burnes and Macnaghten, set a 'mark' on Cabul the memory of which had lasted for decades. Cavagnari and his people had been slaughtered in the Balla Hissar, and their bones were still mingled with the smouldering ruins of the Residency. Wise men discerned that the destruction of the fortress followed by a homeward march as swift yet as measured as had been the march of invasion, could not but have made a deep and lasting impression on the Afghans; while the complications, humiliations, and expense of the long futile occupation would have been obviated. Other counsels prevailed. To discover, in a nation virtually accessory as a whole after the fact to the slaughter of the mission, the men on whom lay the suspicion of having been the instigators and the perpetrators of the cruel deed, to accord them a fair trial, and to send to the gallows those on whose hands was found the blood of the massacred mission, was held a more befitting and not less telling course of retributive action than to raze the Balla Hissar and sow its site with salt. Skilfully and patiently evidence was gathered, and submitted to the Military Commission which General Roberts had appointed. This tribunal took cognisance of crimes nominally of two classes. It tried men who were accused of having been concerned in the destruction of the British mission, and those charged with treason in having offered armed resistance to the British troops acting in support of the Ameer, who had put himself under their protection. Of the five prisoners first tried, condemned, and duly hanged, two were signal criminals. One of them, the Kotwal or Mayor of Cabul, was proved to have superintended the contumelious throwing of the bodies of the slaughtered Guides of the mission escort into the ditch of the Balla Hissar. Another was proved to have carried away from the wrecked Residency a head believed to have been Cavagnari's, and to have exhibited it on the ridge above the city. The other three and many of those who were subsequently executed, suffered for the crime of 'treason' against Yakoub Khan. Probably there was no Afghan who did not approve of the slaughter of the Envoy, and who would not in his heart have rejoiced at the annihilation of the British force; but it seems strange law and stranger justice to hang men for 'treason' against a Sovereign who had gone over to the enemy. On the curious expedient of temporarily governing in the name of an Ameer who had deserted his post to save his skin, comment would be superfluous. Executions continued; few, however, of the mutinous sepoys who actually took part in the wanton attack on the British Residency had been secured, and it was judged expedient that efforts should be made to capture and punish those against whom there was evidence of that crime, in the shape of the muster-rolls of the regiments now in the possession of the military authorities. It was known that many of the disbanded and fugitive soldiers had returned to their homes in the villages around Cabul, and early in November General Baker took out a force and suddenly encircled the village of Indikee, on the edge of the Chardeh valley--a village reported full of Afghan sepoys. A number of men were brought out by the scared headmen and handed over, answering to their names called over from a list carried by Baker; and other villages in the vicinity yielded a considerable harvest of disbanded soldiers. Before the Commission the prisoners made no attempt to conceal their names, or deny the regiments to which they had belonged; and forty-nine of them were found guilty and hanged, nearly all of whom belonged to the regiments that had assailed the Residency.

On 12th November Sir Frederick Roberts proclaimed an amnesty in favour of all who had fought against the British troops, on condition that they should surrender their arms and return to their homes; but exempted from the benefit were all concerned in the attack on the Residency. The amnesty was well timed, although most people would have preferred that fewer sepoys and more Sirdars should have been hanged.

Our relations with the Ameer during the earlier part of his residence in the British camp were not a little peculiar. Nominally he was our guest, and a certain freedom was accorded to him and his retinue. There was no doubt that the Sirdars of the Ameer's suite grossly abused their privileges. Whether with Yakoub Khan's cognisance or not, they authorised the use of his name by the insurgent leaders. Nek Mahomed, the insurgent commander at Charasiah, was actually in the tents of the Ameer on the evening before the fight. To all appearance our operations continued to have for their ultimate object the restoration of Yakoub Khan to his throne. Our administrative measures were carried on in his name. The hostile Afghans we designated as rebels against his rule; and his authority was proclaimed as the justification of much of our conduct. But the situation gradually became intolerable to Yakoub Khan. He was a guest in the British camp, but he was also in a species of custody. Should our arms reinstate him, he could not hope to hold his throne. His harassed perplexity came to a crisis on the morning of the 12th October, the day of General Roberts' durbar in the Balla Hissar, which he had been desired to attend. What he specifically apprehended is unknown; what he did was to tell General Roberts, with great excitement, that he would not go to the durbar, that his life was too miserable for long endurance, that he would rather be a grass-cutter in the British camp than remain Ameer of Afghanistan. He was firmly resolved to resign the throne, and begged that he might be allowed to do so at once. General Roberts explained that the acceptance of his resignation rested not with him but with the Viceroy, pending whose decision matters, the General desired, should remain as they were, affairs continuing to be conducted in the Ameer's name as before. To this the Ameer consented; his tents were moved to the vicinity of General Roberts' headquarters, and a somewhat closer surveillance over him was maintained.

Secrecy meanwhile was preserved until the Viceroy's reply should arrive. The nature of that reply was intimated by the proclamation which General Roberts issued on the 28th October. It announced that the Ameer had of his own free will abdicated his throne and left Afghanistan without a government. 'The British Government,' the proclamation continued, 'now commands that all Afghan authorities, chiefs, and sirdars, do continue their functions in maintaining order . . . . The British Government, after consultation with the principal sirdars, tribal chiefs, and others representing the interests and wishes of the various provinces and cities, will declare its will as to the future permanent arrangements to be made for the good government of the people.'

This *ad interim* assumption of the rulership of Afghanistan may have been adopted as the only policy which afforded even a remote possibility of tranquillity. But it was essentially a policy of speculative makeshift. The retributive and punitive object of the swift march on Cabul can scarcely be regarded as having been fulfilled by the execution of a number of subordinate participants and accessories in the destruction of the mission and by the voluntary abdication of Yakoub Khan. That the Afghan 'authorities, chiefs, and sirdars,' would obey the command to 'maintain order' issued by the leader of a few thousand hostile troops, masters of little more than the ground on which they were encamped, experience and common sense seemed alike to render improbable. The Afghans subordinated their internal quarrels to their common hatred of the masterful foreigners, and the desperate fighting of December proved how fiercely they were in earnest.

Yakoub Khan had been regarded as merely a weak and unfortunate man, but the shadows gradually darkened around him until at length he came to be a man under grave suspicion. General Roberts became satisfied from the results of the proceedings of the court of inquiry, that the attack on the Residency, if not actually instigated by him, might at least have been checked by active exertion on his part. Information was obtained which convinced the General that the ex-Ameer was contemplating a flight toward

Battle Dhoolies

Turkestan, and it was considered necessary to place him in close confinement. He remained a close prisoner until December 1st. On the early morning of that day he was brought out from his tent, and after taking farewell of the General and his staff, started on his journey to Peshawur, surrounded by a strong escort. If the hill tribes along his route had cared enough about him to attempt his rescue, the speed with which he travelled afforded them no time to gather for that purpose.

During those uneventful October and November days, when the little army commanded by General Roberts lay in its breezy camp on the Siah Sung heights, there was no little temptation for the unprofessional reader of the telegraphic information in the newspapers to hold cheap those reputedly formidable Afghans, whose resistance a single sharp skirmish had seemingly scattered to the winds, and who were now apparently accepting without active remonstrance the dominance of the few thousand British bayonets glittering there serenely over against the once turbulent but now tamed hill capital. One may be certain that the shrewd and careful soldier who commanded that scant array did not permit himself to share in the facile optimism whether on the part of a government or of the casual reader of complacent telegrams. It was true that the Government of India had put or was putting some 30,000 soldiers into the field on the apparent errand of prosecuting an Afghan war. But what availed Roberts this host of fighting men when he had to realise that, befall him what might in the immediate or near future, not a man of it was available to strengthen or to succour him? The quietude of those cool October days was very pleasant, but the chief knew well how precarious and deceitful was the calm. For the present the Afghan unanimity of hostility was affected in a measure by the fact that the Ameer, who had still a party, was voluntarily in the British camp. But when Yakoub's abdication should be announced, he knew the Afghan nature too well to doubt that the tribal blood-feuds would be soldered for the time, that Dooranee and Barakzai would strike hands, that Afghan regulars and Afghan irregulars would rally under the same standards, and that the fierce shouts of 'Deen! deen!' would resound on hill-top and in plain. Cut loose from any base, with slowly dwindling strength, with waning stock of ammunition, it was his part to hold his ground here for the winter, he and his staunch soldiers, a firm rock in the midst of those surging Afghan billows that were certain to rise around him. Not only would he withstand them, but he would meet them, for this bold man knew the value in dealing with Afghans of a resolute and vigorous offensive. But it behoved him above all things to make timely choice of his winter quarters where he should collect his supplies and house his troops and the followers. After careful deliberation the Sherpur cantonment was selected. It was over-large for easy defence, but hard work, careful engineering, and steadfast courage would redeem that evil. And Sherpur had the great advantage that besides being in a measure a ready-made defensive position, it had shelter for all the European troops and most of the native soldiery, and that it would accommodate also the horses of the cavalry, the transport animals, and all the needful supplies and stores.

An Afghan of the Afghans, Shere Ali nevertheless had curiously failed to discern that the warlike strength of the nation which he ruled lay in its intuitive aptitude for irregular fighting; and he had industriously set himself to the effort of warping the combative genius of his people and of constituting Afghanistan a military power of the regular and disciplined type. He had created a large standing army the soldiery of which wore uniforms, underwent regular drill, obeyed words of command, and carried arms of precision. He had devoted great pains to the manufacture of a formidable artillery, and what with presents from the British Government and the imitative skill of native artificers he was possessed at the outbreak of hostilities of several hundred cannon. His artisans were skillful enough to turn out in large numbers very fair rifled small-arms, which they copied from British models; and in the Balla Hissar magazine were found by our people vast quantities of gunpowder and of admirable cartridges of local manufacture. There were many reasons why the Cabul division of Shere Ali's army should be quartered apart from his turbulent and refractory capital, and why its cantonment should take the form of a permanent fortified camp, in which his soldiers might be isolated from Cabul intrigues, while its proximity to the capital should constitute a standing menace to the conspirators of the city. His original design apparently was to enclose the Behmaroo heights within the walls of his cantonment, and thus form a great fortified square upon the heights in the centre of which should rise a strong citadel dominating the plain in every direction. The Sherpur cantonment as found by Roberts consisted of a fortified enciente, enclosing on two sides a great open space in the shape of a parallelogram lying along the southern base of the Behmaroo heights. When the British troops took possession, only the west and south faces of the enciente were completed; although not long built those were already in bad repair, and the explosion of the great magazine when the Afghan troops abandoned the cantonment had wrecked a section of the western face. The eastern face had been little more than traced, and the northern side had no artificial protection, but was closed in by the Behmaroo heights, whose centre was cleft by a broad and deep gorge. The design of the enciente was peculiar. There was a thick and high exterior wall of mud, with a banquette for infantry protected by a parapet. Inside this wall was a dry ditch forty feet wide, on the inner brink of which was the long range of barrack-rooms. Along the interior front of the barrack-rooms was a verandah faced with arches supported by pillars, its continuity broken occasionally by broad staircases conducting to the roof of the barracks, which afforded a second line of defence. The closing in of the verandah would of course give additional barrack accommodation, but there were quarters in the barrack-rooms for at least all the European troops. In the southern face of the enciente were three gateways, and in the centre of the western face there was a fourth, each gate covered adequately by a curtain. Between each gate were semicircular bastions for guns. In the interior there was space to manoeuvre a division of all arms. There was a copious supply of water, and if the aspect of the great cantonment was grim because of the absence of trees and the utter barrenness of the enclosed space, this aesthetic consideration went for little against its manifest advantages as snug and defensible winter quarters. Shere Ali had indeed been all unconsciously a friend in need to the British force wintering in the heart of that unfortunate potentate's dominions. Human nature is perverse and exacting, and there were those who objurgated his memory because he had constructed his cantonment a few sizes too large to be comfortably defended by Sir Frederick Roberts' little force. But this was manifestly unreasonable; and in serious truth the Sherpur cantonment was a real godsend to our people. Supplies of all kinds were steadily being accumulated there, and the woodwork of the houses in the Balla Hissar was being carried to Sherpur for use as firewood. On the last day of October the force quitted the Siah Sung position and took possession of Sherpur, which had undergone a rigorous process of fumigation and cleansing. The change was distinctly for the better.

The force was compacted, and the routine military duties were appreciably lightened since there were needed merely piquets on the Behmaroo heights and sentries on the gates; the little army was healthy, temperate, and in excellent case in all respects.

The dispositions for field service made at the outset of the campaign by the military authorities have already been detailed. Regarded simply as dispositions they left nothing to be desired, and certainly Sir Frederick Roberts' force had been organised and equipped with a fair amount of expedition. But it was apparent that the equipment of that body of 6500 men--and that equipment by no means of an adequate character, had exhausted for the time the resources of the Government as regarded transport and supplies. Promptitude of advance on the part of the force to which had been assigned the line of invasion by the Khyber-Jellalabad route, was of scarcely less moment than the rapidity of the stroke which Roberts was commissioned to deliver. The former's was a treble duty. One of its tasks was to open up and maintain Roberts' communications with India, so that the closing of the Shutargurdan should not leave him isolated. Another duty resting on the Khyber force was to constitute for Roberts a ready and convenient reserve, on which he might draw when his occasions demanded. No man could tell how soon after the commencement of his invasion that necessity might arise; it was a prime *raison d'être* of the Khyber force to be in a position to give him the hand when he should intimate a need for support. Yet again, its presence in the passes dominantly thrusting forward, would have the effect of retaining the eastern tribes within their own borders, and hindering them from joining an offensive combination against the little force with which Roberts was to strike at Cabul. But delay on delay marked the mobilisation and advance of the troops operating in the

Khyber line. There was no lack of earnestness anywhere; the eagerness to push on was universal from the commander to the corporal. But the barren hills and rugged passes could furnish no supplies; the base had to furnish everything, and there was nothing at the base, neither any accumulation of supplies nor means to transport supplies if they had been accumulated. Weeks elapsed before the organisation of the force approached completion, and it was only by a desperate struggle that General Charles Gough's little brigade received by the end of September equipment sufficient to enable that officer to advance by short marches. Roberts was holding his durbar in the Balla Hissar of Cabul on the day that the head of Gough's advance reached Jellalabad. No man can associate the idea of dawdling with Jenkins and his Guides, yet the Guides reaching Jellalabad on October 12th were not at Gundamuk until the 23rd, and Gundamuk is but thirty miles beyond Jellalabad. The anti-climax for the time of General Bright's exertions occurred on November 6th. On that day he with Gough's brigade reached so far Cabulward as Kutti Sung, two marches beyond Gundamuk. There he met General Macpherson of Roberts' force, who had marched down from Cabul with his brigade on the errand of opening communications with the head of the Khyber column. The two brigades had touch of each other for the period of an interview between the Generals, and then they fell apart and the momentary union of communication was disrupted. General Bright had to fall back toward Gundamuk for lack of supplies. The breach continued open only for a few days, and then it was closed, not from down country but from up country. Roberts, surveying the rugged country to the east of Cabul, had discerned that the hill road toward Jugdulluk by Luttabund, was at once opener and shorter than the customary tortuous and overhung route through the Khoord Cabul Pass and by Tezeen. The pioneers were set to work to improve the former. The Lut-tabund road became the habitual route along which, from Cabul downwards, were posted detachments maintaining the communications of the Cabul force with the Khyber column and India. Nearly simultaneous with this accomplishment was the accordance to Sir Frederick Roberts of the local rank of Lieutenant-General, a promotion which placed him in command of all the troops in Eastern Afghanistan down to Jumrood, and enabled him to order up reinforcements from the Khyber column at his discretion, a power he refrained from exercising until the moment of urgent need was impending.

After his interview at Kutti Sung with General Bright, Macpherson, before returning to Cabul, made a short reconnaissance north of the Cabul river toward the Lughman valley and into the Tagao country inhabited by the fanatic tribe of the Safis. From his camp at Naghloo a foraging party, consisting of a company of the 67th escorting a number of camels and mules, moved westward toward a village near the junction of the Panjshir and Cabul rivers, there to obtain supplies of grain and forage. The little detachment on its march was suddenly met by the fire of about 1000 Sari tribesmen. Captain Poole, observing that the tribesmen were moving to cut him off, withdrew his party through a defile in his rear, and taking cover under the river bank maintained a steady fire while the camels were being retired. The Safis were extremely bold and they too shot very straight. Captain Poole was severely wounded and of his handful of fifty-six men eight were either killed or wounded, but their comrades resolutely held their position until reinforcements came out from the camp. The Safis, who retired with dogged reluctance, were not finally routed until attacked by British infantry in front and flank. After they broke the cavalry pursued them for six miles, doing severe execution; the dead of the 67th were recovered, but the poor fellows had been mutilated almost past recognition. General Macpherson returned to Sherpur on the 20th November, having left a strong garrison temporarily at Luttabund to strengthen communications and open out effectually the new route eastward.

General Roberts, with all his exertions, had been unable to accumulate sufficient winter of grain for his native troops and forage for his cavalry and baggage animals. Agents had been purchasing supplies in the fertile district of Maidan, distant from Cabul about twenty-five miles in the Ghuznee direction, but the local people lacked carriage to convey their stocks into camp, and it was necessary that the supplies should be brought in by the transport of the force. The country toward Ghuznee was reported to be in a state of disquiet, and a strong body of troops was detailed under the command of General Baker for the protection of the transport. This force marched out from Sherpur on November 21st, and next day camped on the edge of the pleasant Maidan plain. Baker encountered great difficulties in collecting supplies. The villages readily gave in their tribute of grain and forage, but evinced extreme reluctance to furnish the additional quantities which our necessities forced us to requisition. With the villagers it was not a question of money; the supplies for which Baker's commissaries demanded money in hand constituted their provision for the winter season. But the stern maxim of war is that soldiers must live although villagers starve, and this much may be said in our favour that we are the only nation in the world which, when compelled to resort to forced requisitions, invariably pays in hard cash and not in promissory notes. Baker's ready-money tariff was far higher than the current rates, but nevertheless he had to resort to strong measures. In one instance he was defied outright.

A certain Bahadur Khan inhabiting a remote valley in the Bamian direction, refused to sell any portion of his great store of grain and forage, and declined to comply with a summons to present himself in Baker's camp. It was known that he was under the influence of the aged fanatic Moulla the Mushk-i-Alum, who was engaged in fomenting a tribal rising, and it was reported that he was affording protection to a number of the fugitive sepoys of the ex-Ameer's army. A political officer with two squadrons of cavalry was sent to bring into camp the recalcitrant Bahadur Khan. His fort and village were found prepared for a stubborn defence. Received with a heavy fire from a large body of men while swarms of hostile tribesmen showed themselves on the adjacent hills, the horsemen had to withdraw. It was judged necessary to punish the contumacious chief and to disperse the tribal gathering before it should make more head, and Baker led out a strong detachment in light marching order. There was no fighting, and the only enemies seen were a few tribesmen, who drew off into the hills as the head of Baker's column approached. Fort, villages, and valley were found utterly deserted. There were no means to carry away the forage and grain found in the houses, so the villages belonging to Bahadur Khan were destroyed by fire. Their inhabitants found refuge in the surrounding villages, and there was absolutely no foundation for the statements which appeared in English papers to the effect that old men, women, and children were turned out to die in the snow. In the words of Mr Hensman, a correspondent who accompanied the column: 'There were no old men, women, and children, and there was no snow.' British officers cannot be supposed to have found pleasure, on the verge of the bitter Afghan winter, in the destruction of the hovels and the winter stores of food belonging to a number of miserable villagers; but experience has proved that only by such stern measures is there any possibility of cowing the rancour of Afghan tribesmen. No elation can accompany an operation so pitiless, and the plea of stern necessity must be advanced alike and accepted with a shudder. Of the necessity of some such form of reprisals an example is afforded in an experience which befell General Baker a few days later in this same Maidan region. He visited the village of Beni-Badam with a small cavalry escort. The villagers with every demonstration of friendliness entertained the officers and men with milk and fruit, and provided corn and forage for their horses. There were only old men in the village with the women and children, but no treachery was suspected until suddenly two large bodies of armed men were seen hurrying to cut off the retreat, and it was only by hard fighting that the General with his escort succeeded in escaping from the snare. Next day he destroyed the village. Baker probably acted on general principles, but had he cared for precedents he would have found them in the conduct of the Germans in the Franco-Prussian war. He remained in the Maidan district until the transport of the army had brought into Sherpur all the supplies which he had succeeded in obtaining in that region, and then returned to the cantonment.

By the terms of the proclamation which he issued on the 28th October Sir Frederick Roberts was announced as the dominant authority for the time being in Eastern and Northern Afghanistan. He occupied this position just as far as and no further than he could make it good. And he could make it good only over a very circumscribed area. Even more than had been true of Shah Soojah's government forty years previously was it true of Roberts' government now that it was a government of sentry-boxes. He was firm master of the Sherpur cantonment. General Hills, his nominee, held a somewhat precarious sway in Cabul in

Afghan Tribesmen

the capacity of its Governor, maintaining his position there in virtue of the bayonets of his military guard, the support of the adjacent Sherpur, and the waiting attitude of the populace of the capital. East of Cabul the domination of Britain was represented by a series of fortified posts studding the road to Gundamuk, whence to Jumrood the occupation was closer, although not wholly undisturbed. When a column marched out from Sherpur the British power was dominant only within the area of its fire zone. The stretch of road it vacated as it moved on ceased to be territory over which the British held dominion. This narrowly restricted nature of his actual sway Sir Frederick Roberts could not but recognise, but how with a force of 7000 men all told was it possible for him to enlarge its borders? One expedient suggested itself which could not indeed extend the area of his real power, but which might have the effect, to use a now familiar expression, of widening the sphere of his influence. From among the Sirdars who had regarded it as their interest to cast in their lot with the British, he selected four to represent him in the capacity of governors of provinces which his bayonets were not long enough to reach. The experiment made it disagreeably plain that the people of the provinces to which he had deputed governors were utterly indisposed to have anything to do either with them or with him. The governors went in no state, they had no great sums to disburse, they were protected by no armed escorts, and they were regarded by the natives much as the Southern states of the American Union after the Civil War regarded the 'carpet bag' governors whom the North imposed upon them. The Logur Governor was treated with utter contempt. The Kohistanees despitefully used Shahbaz Khan, and when a brother of Yakoub Khan was sent to use his influence in favour of the worried and threatened governor, he was reviled as a 'Kafir' and a 'Feringhee,' and

ordered peremptorily back to Sherpur if he had any regard for his life. Sirdar Wali Mahomed, the governor-nomi-
nate to the remote Turkestan, found pretext after pretext
for delaying to proceed to take up his functions, and had
never quitted the British camp. When Baker returned from
Maidan he reported that he had left the district peaceful
in charge of the governor whom he had installed, the ven-
erable and amiable Hassan Khan. Baker's rear-guard was
scarcely clear of the valley when a mob of tribesmen and
sepoys attacked the fort in which the old Sirdar was re-
siding, shot him through the head, and then hacked his
body to pieces. It was too clear that governors unsupported
by bayonets, and whose only weapons were tact and per-
suasiveness, were at an extreme discount in the condition
which Afghanistan presented in the end of November and
the beginning of December.

CHAPTER 4

The December Storm

The invader of Afghanistan may count as inevitable a national rising against him, but the Afghans are a people so immersed in tribal quarrels and domestic blood feuds that the period of the outbreak is curiously uncertain. The British force which placed Shah Soojah on the throne and supported him there, was in Afghanistan for more than two years before the waves of the national tempest rose around it. The national combination against Roberts' occupation was breaking its strength against the Sherpur defences while as yet the Cabul field force had not been within sight of the capital for more than two months. There seems no relation between opportunity and the period of the inevitable outburst. If in November 1841 the Cabul Sirdars had restrained themselves for a few days longer two more regiments would have been following on Sale's track, and the British force in the cantonments would have been proportionately attenuated. Roberts might have been assailed with better chance of success when his force was dispersed between the Siah Sung camp, the Balla Hissar, and Sherpur, than when concentrated in the strong defensive position against which the Afghans beat in vain. Perhaps the rising ripened faster in 1879 than in 1841 because in the former period no Macnaghten fomented intrigues and scattered gold. Perhaps Shere Ali's military innovations may have instilled into the masses of his time some rough lessons in the art and practice of speedy mobilisation. The crowning disgrace of 1842 was that a trained army of regular soldiers should have been annihilated by a few thousand hillmen, among whom there was no symptom either of real valour or of good leadership. To Roberts and his force attaches the credit of having defeated the persistent and desperate efforts of levies at least ten times superior in numbers, well armed, far from undisciplined, courageous beyond all experience of Afghan nature, and under the guidance of a leader who had some conception of strategy, and who certainly was no mean tactician.

In the Afghan idiosyncrasy there is a considerable strain of practical philosophy. The blood of the massacred mission was not dry when it was recognised in Cabul that stern retribution would inevitably follow. Well, said the Afghans among themselves, what must be must be, for they are all fatalists. The seniors recalled the memory of the retribution Pollock exacted--how he came, destroyed Istalif, set a 'mark' on Cabul by sending the great bazaar in fragments into the air, and then departed. This time Istalif was not compromised; if Roberts Sahib should be determined to blow up the Char Chowk again, why, that infliction must be endured. It had been rebuilt after Pollock Sahib's engineers had worked their will on it; it could be rebuilt a second time when Roberts Sahib should have turned his back on the city, as pray God and the Prophet he might do with no more delay than Pollock Sahib had made out yonder on the Logur plain. So after a trial of Roberts' mettle at Charasiah, and finding the testing sample not quite to their taste, the Afghans fell into an attitude of expectancy, and were mightily relieved by his proclamation read at the Balla Hissar durbar of October 12th. After a reasonable amount of hanging and the exaction of the fine laid on the city, it was assumed that he would no doubt depart so as to get home to India before the winter snows should block the passes. But the expected did not happen. The British General established a British Governor in Cabul who had a heavy hand, and policed the place in a fashion that stirred a lurid fury in the bosoms of haughty Sirdars who had been wont to do what seemed good in their own eyes. He engaged in the sacrilegious work of dismantling the Balla Hissar, the historic fortress of the nation, within whose walls were the royal palace and the residences of the principal nobles. Those were bitter things, but they could be borne if they were mere temporary inflictions, and if the hated Feringhees would but take themselves away soon. But that hope was shattered by the proclamation of October 28th, when the abdication of the Ameer was intimated and the British *raj* in Afghanistan was announced. Yes, that pestilent *zabardasti* little General, who would not follow the example of good old Pollock Sahib, and who held Yakoub Khan and sundry of his Sirdars in close imprisonment in his camp, had now the insolence to proclaim himself virtually the Ameer of Afghanistan! Far from showing symptom of budging, he was sending out his governors into the provinces, he was gathering tribute in kind, and he had taken possession of Shere Ali's monumental cantonment, under the shadow of the Behmaroo heights on which Afghan warriors of a past generation had slaughtered the Feringhee soldiers as if they had been sheep; and it was the Feringhee General's cantonment now, which he was cunningly strengthening as if he meant to make it his permanent fortress.

Yakoub Khan had gained little personal popularity during his brief and troubled reign, but he was an Afghan and a Mahomedan; and his deportation to India, followed shortly afterwards by that of his three Ministers, intensified the rancour of his countrymen and co-religionists against the handful of presumptuous foreigners who arrogantly claimed to sway the destinies of Afghanistan. *Cherchez la femme* is the keynote among Western peoples of an investigation into the origin of most troubles and strifes; the watchword of the student of the springs of great popular outbursts among Eastern nations must be *cherchez les prêtres*. The Peter the Hermit of Afghanistan was the old Mushk-i-Alum, the fanatic Chief Moulla of Ghuznee. This aged enthusiast went to and fro among the tribes proclaiming the sacred duty of a Jehad or religious war against the unbelieving invaders, stimulating the pious passions of the followers of the Prophet by fervent appeals, enjoining the chiefs to merge their intestine strifes in the common universal effort to crush the foreign invaders of the Afghan soil. The female relatives of the abdicated Ameer fomented the rising by appeals to popular sympathy, and by the more practical argument of lavish distribution of treasure. The flame spread, tribesmen and disbanded soldiers sprang to arms, the banner of the Prophet was unfurled, and the nation heaved with the impulse of fanaticism. Musa Khan, the boy heir of Yakoub, was in the hands of the Mushk-i-Alum, and the combination of fighting tribes found a competent leader in Mahomed Jan, a Warduk general of proved courage and capacity. The plan of campaign was comprehensive and well devised. The contingent from the country to the south of the capital, from Logur, Zurmat, and the Mangal and Jadran districts, was to seize that section of the Cabul ridge extending from Charasiah northward to the cleft through which flows the Cabul river. The northern contingent from the Kohistan and Kohdaman was to occupy the Asmai heights and the hills further to the north-west; while the troops from the Maidan and Warduk territories, led by Mahomed Jan in person, were to come in from the westward across the Chardeh valley, take possession of Cabul, and rally to their banners the disaffected population of the capital and the surrounding villages. The concentration of the three bodies effected, the capital and the ridge against which it leans occupied, the next step would be the investment of the Sherpur cantonment, preparatory to an assault upon it in force.

The British general through his spies had information of those projects. To allow the projected concentration to be effected would involve serious disadvantages, and both experience and temperament enjoined on Roberts the offensive. The Logur contingent was regarded as not of much account, and might be headed back by a threat. Mahomed Jan's force, which was reckoned some 5000 strong, needed to be handled with greater vigour. Meer Butcha and his Kohistanees were less formidable, and might be dealt with incidentally. Roberts took a measure of wise precaution in telegraphing to Colonel Jenkins on the 7th December to march his Guides (cavalry and infantry) from Jugdulluk to Sherpur.

On the 8th General Macpherson was sent out toward the west with a column consisting of 1300 bayonets, three squadrons, and eight guns. Following the Ghuznee road across the Chardeh valley, he was to march to Urgundeh, in the vicinity of which place it was expected that he would find Mahomed Jan's levies, which he was to attack and drive backward on Maidan, taking care to prevent their retreat to the westward in the direction of Bamian. On the following day General Baker marched out with a force made up of 900 infantrymen, two and a half squadrons, and four guns, with instructions to march southward toward the Logur valley, deal with the tribal gathering there, then bend sharply in a south-westerly direction and take up a position across the Ghuznee road in the Maidan valley on the line

79

of retreat which it was hoped that Macpherson would succeed in enforcing on Mahomed Jan. In that case the Afghan leader would find himself between two fires, and would be punished so severely as to render it unlikely that he would give further trouble. To afford time for Baker to reach the position assigned to him Macpherson remained halted during the 9th at Aushar, a village just beyond the debouche of the Nanuchee Pass, at the north-western extremity of the Asmai heights. On that day a cavalry reconnaissance discovered that the Kohistanee levies in considerable strength had already gathered about Karez Meer, some ten miles north-west of Cabul, and that masses of Afghans presumably belonging to the force of Mahomed Jan were moving northward in the Kohistan direction, apparently with the object of joining Meer Butcha's gathering at Karez. It was imperative that the latter should be dispersed before the junction could be effected, and Sir Frederick Roberts had no option but to order Macpherson to alter his line of advance and move against the Kohistanees. Necessary as was this divergence from the original plan of operation, it had the effect of sending to wreck the combined movement from which so much was hoped, and of bringing about a very critical situation. If Lockhart's reconnaissance had been made a day earlier, Macpherson might probably have utilised to good purpose by dispersing the Kohistanees, the day which as it was he spent halted at Aushar. He might have accomplished that object equally well if, instead of the cavalry reconnaissance made by Lockhart, Macpherson himself had been instructed to devote the 9th to a reconnaissance in force in the direction of Karez Meer.

The country being held unsuited for the action of wheeled artillery and cavalry, Macpherson left his details of those arms at Aushar, and marched on the morning of the 10th on Karez with his infantry and mountain guns. As his troops crowned the Surkh Kotul they saw before them an imposing spectacle. The whole terrain around Karez swarmed with masses of armed tribesmen, whose banners were flying on every hillock. Down in the Pughman valley to the left rear, were discerned bodies of the hostile contingent from the west, between which and the Kohistanees no junction had fortunately as yet been made. Macpherson's dispositions were simple. His mountain guns shelled with effect the Kohistanee tribesmen, and then he moved forward from the Surkh Kotul in three columns. His skirmishers drove back the forward stragglers, and then the main columns advancing at the double swept the disordered masses before them, and forced them rearward into their intrenched position in front of the Karez village. There the resistance was half-hearted. After a brief artillery preparation the columns carried the position with a rush, and the Kohistanees were routed with heavy loss. Meer Butcha and his Kohistanees well beaten, Macpherson camped for the night near Karez. Baker had reached his assigned position in the Maidan valley, and there seemed a fair prospect that the operation against Mahomed Jan as originally designed might be carried out notwithstanding the interruption to its prosecution which had been found necessary. For there was good reason to believe that the Afghan commander and his force, whose strength was estimated at about 5000 men, were in the vicinity of Urgundeh, about midway between Macpherson at Karez and Baker in the Maidan valley. If Mahomed Jan would be so complaisant as to remain where he was until Macpherson could reach him, then Roberts' strategy would have a triumphant issue, and the Warduk general and his followers might be relegated to the category of negligable quantities.

Orders were sent to Macpherson to march as early as possible on the morning of the 11th, follow up the enemy who had been observed retiring toward the west and south, and endeavour to drive them down toward General Baker. He was further informed that the cavalry and horse-artillery which he had left at Aushar would leave that village at nine A.M. under the command of Brigadier-General Massy, and would cross the Chardeh valley by the Urgundeh road, on which he was directed to join them on his march. The specific instructions given to General Massy were as follows: 'To advance from Aushar by the road leading directly from the city of Cabul toward Urgundeh and Ghuznee' (the main Ghuznee road), 'to proceed cautiously and quietly feeling for the enemy, to communicate with General Macpherson, and to act in conformity with that officer's movements, but on no account to commit himself to an action until General Macpherson had engaged the enemy.'

Macpherson marched at eight A.M., moving in a southwesterly direction toward Urgundeh by a direct track in rear of the range of hills bounding the western edge of the Chardeh valley. To the point at which it was probable that he and Massy should meet he had considerably further to travel than had the latter from the Aushar camp, and Macpherson's force consisted of infantry while that of Massy was cavalry and horse-artillery. Massy left Aushar at nine A.M. in consideration of the shorter distance he had to traverse, and he headed for Killa Kazee, a village near the foothills of the western ridge about four miles from Aushar as the crow flies. He did not comply with the letter of his instructions to follow the Ghuznee road because of the wide detour marching by it would have involved, but instead made his way straight across country. That he should have done this was unfortunate, since the time he thus gained threw him forward into a position involving danger in advance of any possible co-operation on the part of Macpherson, who was still far away from the point of

Bengal Lancers

intended junction while Massy was comparatively near it. Massy's force consisted of two squadrons 9th Lancers and a troop of 14th Bengal Lancers, escorting four horse-artillery guns. He had detached a troop of 9th Lancers to endeavour to open communication with Macpherson, in compliance with his instructions. As he approached Killa Kazee, Captain Gough commanding the troop of 9th Lancers forming the advance guard, sent back word that the hills on either side of the Ghuznee road some distance beyond the village were occupied by the enemy in considerable force. Massy, in his unsupported condition and destitute of any information as to Macpherson's whereabouts, would have shown discretion by halting on receipt of this intelligence pending further developments. But he probably believed that the Afghans flanking the road were casual tribesmen from the adjacent villages who were unlikely to make any stand, and he determined to move on.

What he presently saw gave him pause. A great mass of Afghans some 2000 strong were forming across the Ghuznee road. From the hills to right and left broad streams of armed men were pouring down the hillslopes and forming on the plain. The surprise was complete, the situation full of perplexity. That gathering host in Massy's front could be none other than Mahomed Jan's entire force. So far from being in retreat southward and westward, so far from waiting supinely about Urgundeh until Macpherson as per programme should drive it on to the muzzles of Baker's Martinis, here it was inside our guard, in possession of the interior line, its front facing toward turbulent Cabul and depleted Sherpur, with no obstruction in its path save this handful of lancers and these four guns! Massy's orders, it was true, were to act in conformity with Macpherson's movements, and on no account to commit himself to an action until that officer had engaged the enemy. Yes, but could the framer of those orders have anticipated the possibility of such a position as that in which Massy now found himself? There was no Macpherson within ken of the perplexed cavalryman, nor the vaguest indication of his movements. The enemy had doubled on that stout and shrewd soldier; it was clear that for the moment he was not within striking distance of his foe, whether on flank or on rear. No course of action presented itself to Massy that was not fraught with grave contingencies. If he should keep to the letter of his orders, the Afghan host might be in Cabul in a couple of hours. Should he retire slowly, striving to retard the Afghan advance by his cannon fire and by the threatening demonstrations of his cavalry, the enemy might follow him up so vigorously as to be beyond Macpherson's reach when that officer should make good his point in the direction of Urgundeh. If on the other hand he should show a bold front, and departing from his orders in the urgent crisis face to face with which he found himself should strain every nerve to 'hold' the Afghan masses in their present position, there was the possibility that, at whatever sacrifice to himself and his little force, he might save the situation and gain time for Macpherson to come up and strike Mahomed Jan on flank and in rear.

For better or for worse Massy committed himself to the rasher enterprise, and opened fire on the swiftly growing Afghan masses. The first range was held not sufficiently effective, and in the hope by closer fire of deterring the enemy from effecting the formation they were attempting, the guns were advanced to the shorter ranges of 2500 and 2000 yards. The shells did execution, but contrary to precedent did not daunt the Afghans. They made good their formation under the shell fire. Mahomed Jan's force had been estimated of about 5000 strong; according to Massy's estimate it proved to be double that number. The array was well led; it never wavered, but came steadily on with waving banners and loud shouts. The guns had to be retired; they came into action again, but owing to the rapidity of the Afghan advance at shorter range than before. The carbine fire of thirty dismounted lancers 'had no appreciable effect.' The outlook was already ominous when at this moment Sir Frederick Roberts came on the scene. As was his wont, he acted with decision. The action, it was clear to him, could not be maintained against odds so overwhelming and in ground so unfavourable. He immediately ordered Massy to retire slowly, to search for a road by which the guns could be withdrawn, and to watch for an opportunity to execute a charge under cover of which the guns might be extricated. He despatched an aide-de-camp in quest of Macpherson, with an order directing that officer to wheel to his left into the Chardeh valley and hurry to Massy's assistance; and he ordered General Hills to gallop to Sherpur and warn General Hugh Gough, who had charge in the cantonment, to be on the alert, and also to send out at speed a wing of the 72d to the village of Deh Mazung, in the throat of the gorge of the Cabul river, which the Highlanders were to hold to extremity.

The enemy were coming on, the guns were in imminent danger, and the moment had come for the action of the cavalry. The gallant Cleland gave the word to his lancers and led them straight for the centre of the Afghan line, the troop of Bengal Lancers following in support. Gough, away on the Afghan left, saw his chief charging and he eagerly 'conformed,' crushing in on the enemy's flank at the head of his troop. 'Self-sacrifice' the Germans hold the duty of cavalry; and there have been few forlorner hopes than the errand on which on this ill-starred day our 200 troopers rode into the heart of 10,000 Afghans flushed with unwonted good fortune. Through the dust-cloud of the charge were visible the flashes of the Afghan volleys and the sheen of the British lance heads as they came down to the 'engage.' There was a short interval of suspense, the stour and bicker of the mêlée faintly heard, but invisible behind the bank of smoke and dust. Then from out the cloud of battle riderless horses came galloping back, followed by broken groups of troopers. Gallantly led home, the charge had failed--what other result could have been expected? Its career had been blocked by sheer weight of opposing numbers. Sixteen troopers had been killed, seven were wounded, two officers had been slain in the hand-to-hand strife. Cleland came out with a sword cut and a bullet wound. Captain Stewart Mackenzie had been crushed under his fallen horse, but distinguished himself greatly, and brought the regiment out of action. As the dust settled it was apparent that the charge had merely encouraged the enemy, who as they steadily pressed on in good order, were waving their banners in triumph and brandishing their tulwars and knives. The fire from the Sniders and Enfields of their marksmen was well directed and deliberate. While Cleland's broken troopers were being rallied two guns were brought into action, protected in a measure by Gough's troop and the detachment of Bengal Lancers, which had not suffered much in the charge. But the Afghans came on so ardently that there was no alternative but prompt retreat. One gun had to be spiked and abandoned, Lieutenant Hardy of the Horse Artillery remaining by it until surrounded and killed. Some 500 yards further back, near the village of Baghwana, the three remaining guns stuck fast in a deep watercourse. At General Roberts' instance a second charge was attempted, to give time for their extrication; but it made no head, so that the guns had to be abandoned, and the gunners and drivers with their teams accompanied the retirement of the cavalry. Some fugitives both of cavalry and artillery hurried to the shelter of the cantonment somewhat precipitately; but the great majority of Massy's people behaved well, rallying without hesitation and constituting the steady and soldierly little body with which Roberts, retiring on Deh Mazung as slowly as possible to give time for the Highlanders from Sherpur to reach that all-important point, strove to delay the Afghan advance. This in a measure was accomplished by the dismounted fire of the troopers, and the retirement was distinguished by the steady coolness displayed by Gough's men and Neville's Bengal Lancers. Deh Mazung was reached, but no Highlanders had as yet reached that place. The carbines of the cavalrymen were promptly utilised from the cover the village afforded; but they could not have availed to stay the Afghan rush. There was a short interval of extreme anxiety until the 200 men of the 72d, Brownlow leading them, became visible advancing at the double through the gorge. 'It was literally touch and go who should reach the village first, the Highlanders or the Afghans,' who were streaming toward it 'like ants on a hill,' but the men of the 72nd swept in, and swarming to the house tops soon checked with their breechloaders the advancing tide. After half-an-hour of futile effort the Afghans saw fit to abandon the attempt to force the gorge, and inclining to their right they occupied the Takht-i-Shah summit, the slopes of the Sher Derwaza heights, and the villages in the south-eastern section of the Chardeh valley.

Macpherson, marching from the Surkh Kotul toward Urgundeh, had observed parties of Afghans crossing his front in the direction of the Chardeh valley, and when the sound reached him of Massy's artillery fire he wheeled to his left through a break in the hills opening into the Chardeh valley, and approached the scene of the discomfiture of Massy's force. This he did at 12.30 P.M., four and a half hours after leaving the Surkh Kotul. As the length of his march was about ten miles, it may be assumed that he encountered difficulties in the rugged track by which he moved, for Macpherson was not the man to linger by the way when there was the prospect of a fight. Had it been possible for him to have marched two hours earlier than he did--and his orders were to march as early as possible--his doing so would have made all the difference in the world to Massy, and could scarcely have failed to change the face of the day. He did not discover the lost guns, but he struck the Afghan rear, which was speedily broken and dispersed by the 67th and 3d Sikhs. Macpherson's intention to spend the night at Killa Kazee was changed by the receipt of an order from General Roberts calling him in to Deh Maz-ung, where he arrived about nightfall. Sir Frederick Rob-erts then returned to Sherpur, for the defence of which General Hugh Gough had made the best dispositions in his power, and the slender garrison of which was to receive in the course of the night an invaluable accession in the shape of the Guides, 900 strong, whom Jenkins had brought up by forced marches from Jugdulluk.

The misfortunes of the day were in a measure retrieved by a well-timed, ready-witted, and gallant action on the part of that brilliant and lamented soldier Colonel Macgre-gor. A wing of the 72nd had been called out to hold the gorge of the Cabul river, but the Nanuchee Pass, through which led the direct road from the scene of the combat to Sherpur, remained open; and there was a time when the Afghan army was heading in its direction. Macgregor had hurried to the open pass in time to rally about him a number of Massy's people, who had lost their officers and were making their way confusedly toward the refuge of Sherpur. Remaining in possession of this important point until all danger was over, he noticed that the ground about

Bagwana, where the guns had been abandoned, was not held by the enemy, and there seemed to him that the opportunity to recover them presented itself. Taking with him a detachment of lancers and artillerymen, he rode out and met with no molestation beyond a few shots from villagers. From Macpherson's baggage guard, met as it crossed the valley toward Sherpur, he requisitioned sixty infantrymen who entered and held Bagwana, and covered him and the gunners during the long and arduous struggle to extricate the guns from their lair in the deep and rugged watercourse. This was at length accomplished, scratch teams were improvised, and the guns, which were uninjured although the ammunition boxes had been emptied, were brought into the cantonment to the general joy.

The result of the day's operations left General Baker momentarily belated. But on the morning of the 11th that officer, finding that no Afghans were being driven down upon him in accordance with the programme, quitted the Maidan country and marched northward toward Urgundeh. An attack on his baggage and rearguard was foiled; but as he reached his camping ground for the night at Urgundeh the Afghans were found in possession of the gorge opening into the Chardeh valley, through which ran his road to Cabul. They were dislodged by a dashing attack of part of the 92nd Highlanders led by Lieutenant Scott Napier. It was not until the morning of the 12th that Baker was informed by heliograph from Sherpur of the occurrences of the previous day, and received directions to return to the cantonment without delay. In the course of a few hours he was inside Sherpur, notwithstanding that his march had been constantly molested by attacks on his rear-guard.

The casualties of the 11th had been after all not very serious. All told they amounted to thirty men killed and forty-four wounded; fifty-one horses killed and sixteen wounded. But the Afghans were naturally elated by the success they had unquestionably achieved; the national rising had been inaugurated by a distinct triumph, the news of which would bring into the field incalculable swarms of fierce and fanatical partisans. It was clear that Mahomed Jan had a quick eye for opportunities, and some skill in handling men. That he could recognise the keypoint of a position and act boldly and promptly on that recognition, his tactics of the 11th made abundantly obvious, and his commanding position on the morning of the 12th still further demonstrated his tactical ability. *L'audace, encore l'audace, et toujours l'audace* is the game to be played by the commander of disciplined troops against Asiatic levies, and no man was more sensible of this than the gallant soldier who now from the bastion of Sherpur could see the Afghan standards waving on the summit of the Takht-i-Shah. Indeed he was impressed so thoroughly by the force of the maxim as to allow himself to hope that some 560 soldiers, of whom about one-third were Europeans, backed by a couple of mountain guns, would be able to carry by assault the lofty peak, strongly held by resolute Afghans in protected positions, supported by several thousands of their fellows lying out of sight until an attack should develop itself, to meet which they were at hand to reinforce the garrison of the Takht-i-Shah. From the gorge of the Cabul river there runs due south to near Charasiah a lofty and rugged range, the highest point of which, the Takht-i-Shah, is about midway from either extremity. From this main ridge there project eastward at right angles two lateral spurs. The shorter and more northerly of those runs down to the Balla Hissar, the longer and more southerly obtruding itself into the plain as far as the village of Beni Hissar. This latter spur quits the main ridge no great distance south of the Takht-i-Shah peak, and on the 12th the Afghan reserves were massed in rear of the peak, both on the main ridge and on this spur. The steep faces of the mountain were strewn with great smooth boulders and jagged masses of rock; the ascent, everywhere laborious, was complicated in places by sheer scarps, and those formidable impediments were made still more difficult by frequent sungahs, strong stone curtains behind which the defenders lay safe or fired with a minimum of exposure. On the summit was a great natural cavity which had been made bomb proof by art, and further cover was afforded by caves and lines of rock. The most northerly portion of the ridge described is known as the Sher Derwaza heights, which Macpherson had occupied on the morning of the 12th, and his brigade it was which furnished the little force already mentioned as charged to attempt the task of storming the Takht-i-Shah.

For several hours Morgan's two mountain guns industriously shelled that peak, and then the infantry made their effort. The Afghans fought stubbornly in defence of a lower hill they held in advance of the Takht-i-Shah, but after a hard struggle they had to abandon it to Macpherson's resolute men. But the exertions of the latter to ascend the peak were baulked by its rugged steepness and the fire of the Afghans holding the sungahs on its face. Sir Frederick Roberts had to recognise that the direct attack by so weak a force unaided by a diversion, could not succeed, and he ordered further efforts to be deferred. The casualties of the abortive attempt included three officers, one of whom, Major Cook, V.C. of the Goorkhas, than whom the British army contained no better soldier, died of his wound. Macpherson was directed to hold the ground he had won, including the lower advanced hill, and was informed that on the following morning he was to expect the co-operation of General Baker from the direction of Beni Hissar.

The lesson of the result of attempting impossibilities had

been taken to heart, and the force which Baker led out on the morning of the 13th was exceptionally strong, consisting as it did of the 92d Highlanders and Guides infantry, a wing of the 3d Sikhs, a cavalry regiment, and eight guns. Marching in the direction of the lateral spur extending from the main ridge eastward to Beni Hissar, Baker observed that large masses of the enemy were quitting the plain villages about Beni Hissar in which they had taken shelter for the night, and were hurrying to gain the summit of the spur which constituted the defensive position of the Afghan reserve. Baker's *coup d'oeil* was quick and true. By gaining the centre of the spur he would cut in two the Afghan line along its summit, and so isolate and neutralise the section of it from the centre to the Beni Hissar extremity, toward which section the reinforcements from the plain villages were climbing. But to accomplish this shrewd stroke it was necessary that he should act with promptitude and energy. His guns opened fire on the summit. The Sikhs, extended athwart the plain, protected his right flank. His cavalry on the left cut into the bodies of Afghans hurrying to ascend the eastern extremity of the spur. With noble emulation the Highlanders and the Guides sprang up the rugged slope, their faces set towards the centre of the summit line. Major White, who already had earned many laurels in the campaign, led on his Highlanders; the Guides, burning to make the most of their first opportunity to distinguish themselves, followed eagerly the gallant chief who had so often led them to victory on other fields. Lieutenant Forbes, a young officer of the 92nd heading the advance of his regiment, reached the summit accompanied only by his colour-sergeant. A band of Ghazees rushed on the pair and the sergeant fell. As Forbes stood covering his body he was overpowered and slain. The sudden catastrophe staggered for a moment the soldiers following their officer, but Lieutenant Dick Cunyngham rallied them immediately and led them forward at speed. For his conduct on this occasion Cunyngham received the Victoria Cross.

With rolling volleys Highlanders and Guides reached and won the summit. The Afghans momentarily clung to the position, but the British fire swept them away and the bayonets disposed of the Ghazees, who fought and died in defence of their standards. The severance of the Afghan line was complete. A detachment was left to maintain the isolation of some 2000 of the enemy who had been cut off; and then swinging to their right Baker's regiments swept along the summit of the spur toward the main ridge and the Takht-i-Shah, the Highlanders leading. As they advanced they rolled up the Afghan line and a panic set in among the enemy, who sought safety in flight. Assailed from both sides, for Macpherson's men from the conical hill were passing up the north side of the peak, and shaken by the steady fire of the mountain guns, the garrison of the Takht-i-Shah evacuated the position. Baker's soldiers toiled vigorously upward toward the peak, keen for the honour of winning it; but the credit of that achievement justly fell to their comrades of Macpherson's command, who had striven so valiantly to earn it the day before, and who had gained possession of the peak and the Afghan standards flying on its summit, a few minutes before the arrival of White's Highlanders and Jenkins' Guides. As the midday gun was fired in the cantonment the flash of the heliograph from the peak told that the Takht-i-Shah was won.

While Baker was sweeping the spur and climbing the lofty peak of the main ridge, his reserve, which remained in the plain, was in sharp action against masses of assailants from the city and other bodies from the villages about Beni Hissar. Those were beaten off by the 3d Sikhs and Baker's flanks were thus cleared, but the resolute Afghans, bent on interfering with his return march, surged away in the direction of the Siah Sung ridge and gathered thereon in considerable strength. The guns of Sherpur shelled them smartly, but they held their ground; and Massy went out to disperse them with the cavalry. The Afghans showed unwonted resolution, confronting the cavalry with extraordinary steadiness in regular formation and withholding their fire until the troopers were close upon them. But the horsemen were not to be denied. Captains Butson and Chisholme led their squadrons against the Afghan flanks, and the troopers of the 9th avenged the mishap which had befallen that gallant regiment two days before, riding through and through the hostile masses and scattering them over the plain. But in the charge Butson was killed, Chisholme and Trower were wounded; the sergeant-major and three men were killed and seven were wounded. Brilliant charges were delivered by the other cavalry detachments, and the Siah Sung heights were ultimately cleared. The Guides' cavalry attacked, defeated, and pursued for a long distance a body of Kohistanees marching from the north-east apparently with intent to join Mahomed Jan. The casualties of the day were sixteen killed and forty-five wounded; not a heavy loss considering the amount of hard fighting. The Afghans were estimated to have lost in killed alone from 200 to 300 men.

The operations of the day were unquestionably successful so far as they went, but the actual results attained scarcely warranted the anticipation that the Afghans would acknowledge themselves defeated by breaking up their combination and dispersing to their homes. It was true that they had been defeated, but they had fought with unprecedented stubbornness and gave little evidence of being cowed. Throughout the day the villages around Cabul had evinced a rancorous hostility which had a marked significance. Not less significant was the participation in the fighting of the day on the part of the population of Cabul. As Baker was returning to Sherpur in the evening he had been fired upon from the Balla Hissar, and his flanking parties had found ambushes of armed Afghans among the willows between the city and the cantonment. But for the skill and courage of the non-commissioned officer in charge a convoy of wounded on its way to Sherpur would certainly have been destroyed. But there was a stronger argument than any of those indications, significant as they were of the unbroken spirit of the Afghans, telling against the probability that the operations of the day would have the effect of putting down the national rising. The hordes which had gathered to the banners of the Mushk-i-Alum and Mahomed Jan combined with the fanaticism of the jehad a fine secular greed for plunder. Was it likely that they would scatter resignedly, leaving untouched the rich booty of the city that had been almost within arm's-length as they looked down on it from the peak of the Takht-i-Shah, and whose minarets they were within sight of on the spur and in the villages of Beni-Hissar? Was that ever likely? And was it not made more and yet more unlikely when on the afternoon of the 13th Macpherson, acting on orders, moved his camp to the Balla Hissar heights, evacuating Deh Mazung and leaving open to the enemy the road into the city through the Cabul gorge? The following morning was to show how promptly and how freely the Afghans had taken advantage of the access to the capital thus afforded them. It must never be forgotten that at this time our people in Afghanistan held no more territory than the actual ground they stood upon and the terrain swept by their fire. No trustworthy intelligence from outside that region was procurable; and of this there can be no clearer evidence than that the General was under the belief that the enemy had been 'foiled in their western and southern operations.'

The morning of the 14th effectually dispelled the optimistic anticipations indulged in overnight. At daybreak a large body of Afghans, with many standards, were discerned on a hill about a mile northward of the Asmai ridge, from which and from the Kohistan road they were moving on to the crest of that ridge. They were joined there by several thousands coming up the slopes from out the village of Deh Afghan, the northern suburb of Cabul. It was estimated that there were about 8000 men in position along the summit of the ridge, and occupying also a low conical hill beyond its north-western termination. The array of Afghans displayed itself within a mile of the west face of the Sherpur cantonment, and formed a menace which could not be brooked. To General Baker was entrusted the task of dislodging the enemy from the threatening position, and there was assigned to him for this purpose a force consisting of about 1200 bayonets, eight guns, and a regiment of native cavalry. His first object was to gain possession of the conical hill already mentioned, and thus debar the Afghan force on the Asmai heights from receiving accessions either from the masses on the hill further north or by the Kohistan road. Under cover of the artillery fire the Highlanders and Guides occupied this conical hill after a short conflict. A detachment was left to hold it and then Colonel Jenkins, who commanded the attack, set about the arduous task of storming from the northward the formidable position of the Asmai heights. The assault was led by Brownlow's staunch Highlanders, supported on the right by the Guides operating on the enemy's flank; and the Afghan position was heavily shelled by four of Baker's guns, and by four more in action near the south-western corner of the Sherpur cantonment. Macpherson from his position on the

Balla Hissar hill aided the attack by the fire of his guns, and also by despatching two companies of the 67th to cross the Cabul gorge and operate against the enemy's left rear.

In the face of a heavy fire the Highlanders and Guides climbed with great speed and steadiness the rugged hillside leading upward to the Afghan breastwork on the northern edge of the summit. Their approach and the crushing shrapnel fire from the guns near Sherpur had caused numerous Afghans to move downward from the position toward Deh Afghan, heavily smitten as they went; but the ghazees in the breastworks made a strenuous resistance and died under their banners as the Highlanders carried the defences with a rush. The crest, about a quarter of a mile long, was traversed under heavy fire and the southern breastwork on the peak was approached. It was strong and strongly held, but a cross fire was brought to bear on its garrison, and then the frontal attack led by a lance-corporal of the 72d was delivered. After a hand-to-hand grapple in which Highlanders and Guides were freely cut and slashed by the knives of the ghazees, the position, which was found full of dead, was carried, but with considerable loss. The whole summit of the Asmai heights was now in British possession, and everything seemed auspicious. The Afghans streaming down from the heights toward the city were being lacerated by shell fire and musketry fire as they descended. When they took refuge in Deh Afghan that suburb was heavily shelled, and it was gradually evacuated.

Scarcely had Jenkins won the summit of the Asmai ridge when the fortune of the day was suddenly overcast; indeed while he was still engaged in the attainment of that object premonitory indications of serious mischief were unexpectedly presenting themselves. A vast host of Afghans described as numbering from 15,000 to 20,000, debouched into the Chardeh valley from the direction of

Indikee, and were moving northwards, apparently with the object of forming a junction with the masses occupying the hills to the north-west of the Asmai heights. About the same time cavalry scouting in the Chardeh valley brought in the information that large parties of hostile infantry and cavalry were hurrying across the valley in the direction of the conical hill the defence of which had been entrusted to Lieutenant-Colonel Clark with 120 Highlanders and Guides. Recognising Clark's weakness, General Baker had judiciously reinforced that officer with four mountain guns and 100 bayonets. The guns opened fire on the Afghan bodies marching from the Killa Kazee direction, and drove them out of range. But they coalesced with the host advancing from Indikee, and the vast mass of Afghans, facing to the right, struck the whole range of the British position from near the Cabul gorge on the south to and beyond the conical hill on the north. The most vulnerable point was the section at and about that eminence, and the necessity for supplying Clark with further reinforcements became urgently manifest. Baker sent up a second detachment, and 200 Sikhs came out from Sherpur at the double. But the Afghans, creeping stealthily in great numbers up the slope from out the Chardeh valley, had the shorter distance to travel, and were beforehand with the reinforcements. Their tactics were on a par with their resolution. The left of their attack grasped and held a knoll north of the conical hill, and from this position of vantage brought a cross fire to bear on Clark's detachment. As their direct attack developed itself it encountered from the conical hill a heavy rifle fire, and shells at short range tore through the loose rush of ghazees, but the fanatics sped on and up without wavering. As they gathered behind a mound for the final onslaught, Captain Spens of the 72d with a handful of his Highlanders went out on the forlorn hope of dislodging them. A rush was made on him; he was overpowered and slaughtered after a desperate resistance, and the Afghan charge swept up the hill-side. In momentary panic the defenders gave ground, carrying downhill with them the reinforcement of Punjaubees which Captain Hall was bringing up. Two of the mountain guns were lost, but there was a rally at the foot of the hill under cover of which the other two were extricated. The Afghans refrained from descending into the plain, and directed their efforts toward cutting off the occupants of the position on the Asmai summit. They ascended by two distinct directions. One body from the conical hill followed the route taken by Jenkins in the morning; another scaled a spur trending downward to the Chardeh valley from the southern extremity of the Asmai ridge.

It was estimated that the Afghan strength disclosed this day did not fall short of 40,000 men; and General Roberts was reluctantly compelled to abandon for the time any further offensive efforts. His reasons, stated with perfect frankness, may best be given in his own words. 'Up to this time,' he wrote, 'I had no reason to apprehend that the Afghans were in sufficient force to cope successfully with disciplined troops, but the resolute and determined manner in which the conical hill had been recaptured, and the information sent to me by Brigadier-General Macpherson that large masses of the enemy were still advancing from the north, south, and west, made it evident that the numbers combined against us were too overwhelming to admit of my comparatively small force meeting them. I therefore determined to withdraw from all isolated positions, and to concentrate the whole force at Sherpur, thus securing the safety of our large cantonment, and avoiding what had now become a useless sacrifice of life.' The orders issued to Generals Baker and Macpherson to retire into the cantonment were executed with skill and steadiness. Jenkins' evacuation of the Asmai position was conspicuously adroit. When the order to quit reached that able officer, Major Stockwell of the 72d was out with a small detachment, maintaining a hot fire on the Afghan bodies ascending by the southern spur from the Chardeh valley. He fell back with great deliberation, and when he rejoined the retirement down the hill face looking toward Sherpur was leisurely proceeded with, the hostile advance from, the northern side being held in check by the fire of covering parties from Jenkins' left flank. General Macpherson's retirement was masterly. Flanking his march through the Cabul gorge with two companies of the 67th who stalled off a rush of ghazees from the Asmai crest, he continued his march through the suburb of Deh Afghan, his baggage in front under a strong guard. Some few shots were exchanged before the suburb was cleared, but the casualties were few and presently the brigade entered the cantonment. General Baker continued to hold a covering position with part of his force, until the troops from the heights and Macpherson's command had made good their retirement, and he was the last to withdraw. By dusk the whole force was safely concentrated within the cantonment, and the period of the defensive had begun. The casualties of the day were serious; thirty-five killed, and 107 wounded. During the week of fighting the little force had lost somewhat heavily; the killed numbered eighty-three, the wounded 192. Eight officers were killed, twelve were wounded.

CHAPTER 5

On the Defensive in Sherpur

Although overlarge for its garrison, the Sherpur cantonment had many of the features of a strong defensive position. On the southern and western faces the massive and
continuous enciente made it impregnable against any force
unprovided with siege artillery. But on the eastern face the
wall had been built to the elevation only of seven feet, and
at either end of the Behmaroo heights, which constituted
the northern line of defence, there were open gaps which
had to be made good. The space between the north-western bastion and the heights was closed by an entrenchment
supported by a 'laager' of Afghan gun-carriages and lim-
bers, the ground in front strengthened by abattis and wire
entanglements, beyond which a village flanking the northern and western faces was occupied as a detached post. The
open space on the north-eastern angle was similarly fortified; the village of Behmaroo was loopholed, and outlying
buildings to the front were placed in a state of defence. The
unfinished eastern wall was heightened by logs built up
in tiers, and its front was covered with abattis, a tower and
garden outside being occupied by a detachment. A series
of block houses had been built along the crest of the Behmaroo heights supporting a continuous entrenchment, gun
emplacements made in the line of defence, and the gorge
dividing the heights strongly fortified against an attack from

the northern plain. The enciente was divided into sections to each of which was assigned a commanding officer with a specified detail of troops; and a strong reserve of European infantry was under the command of Brigadier-General Baker, ready at short notice to reinforce any threatened point. It was presumably owing to the absorption of the troops in fighting, collecting supplies, and providing winter shelter, that when the concentration within Sherpur became suddenly necessary the defences of the position were still seriously defective; and throughout the period of investment the force was unremittingly engaged in the task of strengthening them. Nor had the military precaution been taken of razing the villages and enclosures within the fire zone of the enciente, and they remained to afford cover to the enemy during the period of investment.

Before the enemy cut the telegraph wire in the early morning of the 15th Sir Frederick Roberts had informed the authorities in India of his situation and of his need for reinforcements; and he had also ordered up General Charles Gough's brigade without loss of time. Gough was already at Jugdulluk when he received the order calling him to Cabul, but he had to wait for reinforcements and supplies, and the tribesmen were threatening his position and the line of communication in rear of it. He did not move forward until the 21st. On the following day he reached Luttabund, whence he took on with him the garrison of that post, but although his march was unmolested it was not until the 24th that he reached Sherpur, a day too late to participate in repelling the assault on the cantonment.

While General Roberts' force was busily engaged in making good the defences of Sherpur, the Afghans refrained from attempting to back their success on the Asmai heights by an assault on the defensive position which seemed to invite an attack. During the first two days of their possession of the city they were enjoying the fruits of their occupation in their own turbulent manner. Roberts' spies reported them busily engaged in sacking the Hindoo and Kuzzilbash quarters, in looting and wrecking the houses of chiefs and townsfolk who had shown friendliness to the British, and in quarrelling among themselves over the spoils. Requisitioning was in full force. The old Moulla Mushk-i-Alum was the temporary successor of General Hills in the office of Governor of Cabul; and spite of his ninety years he threw extraordinary energy into the work of arousing fanaticism and rallying to Cabul the fighting men of the surrounding country. The jehad of which he had been the chief instigator had certainly attained unexampled dimensions, and although it was not in the nature of things that every Afghan who carried arms should be inspired with religious fanaticism to such a pitch as to be utterly reckless of his life, swarms of fierce ghazees made formidable the levies which Mahomed Jan commanded.

On the 17th and 18th the Afghans made ostentatious demonstrations against Sherpur, but those were never formidable, although they made themselves troublesome with some perseverance during the daytime, consistently refraining from night attacks, which was remarkable since ordinarily they are much addicted to the chapao . There never was any investment of Sherpur, or indeed any approximation to investment. Cavalry reconnaissances constantly went out, and piquets and videttes were habitually on external duty; infantry detachments sallied forth whenever occasion demanded to dislodge the assailants from points occupied by them in inconvenient proximity to the defences. The Afghan offensive was not dangerous, but annoying and wearying. It was indeed pushed with some resolution on the 18th, when several thousand men poured out of the city, and skirmished forward under cover of the gardens and enclosures on the plain between Cabul and Sherpur, in the direction of the southern front and the south-western bastions. The Afghans are admirable skirmishers, and from their close cover kept up for hours a brisk fire on the soldiers lining the Sherpur defences, but with singularly little effect. The return rifle fire was for the most part restricted to volleys directed on those of the enemy who offered a sure mark by exposing themselves; and shell fire was chiefly used to drive the Afghan skirmishers from their cover in the gardens and enclosures. Some of those, notwithstanding, were able to get within 400 yards of the enciente, but could make no further headway. On the morning of the 19th it was found that in the night the enemy had occupied the Meer Akhor fort, a few hundred yards beyond the eastern face, and close to the Residency compound of the old cantonments of 1839-42. The fire from this fort was annoying, and General Baker went out on the errand of destroying it, with 800 bayonets, two mountain guns, and a party of sappers. As the fort was being approached through the dense mist a sudden volley from it struck down several men, and Lieutenant Montenaro of the mountain battery was mortally wounded. The fort was heavily shelled from the south-eastern bastion; its garrison evacuated it, and it was blown up.

Mahomed Jan and his coadjutors could hardly flatter themselves that as yet they had made any impression on the steadfast defence which the British force was maintaining in the Sherpur cantonment. The Afghan leader had tried force in vain; he knew the history of that strange period in the winter of 1841 during which Afghan truculence and audacity had withered the spirit of a British force not much less numerically strong than the little army now calmly withstanding him. Things had not gone very well with that little army of late, possibly its constancy might have been impaired, and its chief might be willing, as had been Elphinstone and the Eltchi, to listen to terms. Anyhow there could be no harm in making a proffer based on the old lines. So the Afghan leader proposed to General Roberts, apparently in all seriousness, that the British army should forthwith evacuate Afghanistan, encountering no molestation in its march; that the British General before departing should engage that Yakoub Khan should return to Afghanistan as its Ameer; and that there should be left behind two officers of distinction as hostages for the faithful fulfilment of the contract. 'We have a lakh of men; they are like wolves eager to rush on their prey! We cannot much longer control them!'—such were said to have been the terms of a message intended to disturb the equanimity of the British commander. Meer Butcha and his Kohistanees, again, were not to all appearance anxious for the restoration of Yakoub. They professed themselves content to accept our staunch friend Wali Mahomed as Ameer, if only the British army would be good enough to march home promptly and leave to Afghans the administration of Afghan affairs. It was not likely that a man of Roberts' nature would demean himself to take any notice of such overtures. For the moment circumstances had enforced on him the wisdom of accepting the defensive attitude, but he knew himself, nevertheless, the virtual master of the situation. He had but one serious anxiety—the apprehension lest the Afghans should not harden their hearts to deliver an assault on his position.

That apprehension was not long to give him concern. On the 20th, as a menace against the southern face of Sherpur, the enemy took strong possession of the Mahomed Shereef fort, stormed so gallantly by Colonel Griffiths on 6th November 1841; and they maintained themselves there during the two following days in face of the fire of siege guns mounted on the bastions of the enciente. On the 21st and 22d large numbers of Afghans quitted the city, and passing eastward behind the Siah Sung heights, took possession in great force of the forts and villages outside the eastern face of Sherpur. On the 22d a spy brought in the intelligence that Mahomed Jan and his brother-chiefs had resolved to assault the cantonment early on the following morning, and the spy was able to communicate the plan of attack. The 2000 men holding the King's Garden and the Mahomed Shereef fort had been equipped with scaling ladders, and were to make a false attack which might become a real one, against the western section of the southern front. The principal assault, however, was to be made against the eastern face of the Behmaroo village—unquestionably the weakest part of the defensive position. The 23rd was the last day of the Mohurrum—the great Mahomedan religious festival, when fanaticism would be at its height; and further to stimulate that incentive to valour, the Mushk-i-Alum would himself kindle the beacon fire on the Asmai height which was to be the signal to the faithful to rush to the assault.

The information proved perfectly accurate. All night long the shouts and chants of the Afghans filled the air. Purposeful silence reigned throughout the cantonment. In the darkness the soldiers mustered and quietly fell into their places; the officers commanding sections of the defence made their dispositions; the reserves were silently standing to their arms. Every eye was toward the Asmai heights, shrouded still in the gloom of the night. A long tongue of flame shot up into the air, blazed brilliantly for a few moments, and then waned. At the signal a fierce fire opened from the broken ground before one of the gateways of the southern face, the flashes indicating that the marksmen were plying their rifles within 200 yards of the enciente. The bullets sped harmlessly over the defenders sheltered behind the parapet, and in the dusk of the dawn reprisals were not attempted. But this outburst of powder-burning against the southern face was a mere incident; what men listened and watched for was the development of the true assault on the eastern end of the great parallelogram. The section commanders there were General Hugh Gough in charge of the eastern end of the Behmaroo heights, and Colonel Jenkins from the village down to the Native Hospital and beyond to the bastion at the south-eastern corner. The troops engaged were the Guides from the ridge down to Behmaroo village and beyond to the Native Hospital, in which were 100 men of the 28th Punjaub Infantry, and between the Hospital and the corner bastion the 67th, reinforced by two companies of 92d Highlanders from the reserve, which later sent to the defence of the eastern face additional contributions of men and guns. 'From beyond Behmaroo and the eastern trenches and walls,' writes Mr Hensman, 'came a roar of voices so loud and menacing that it seemed as if an army fifty thousand strong was charging down on our thin line of men. Led by their ghazees, the main body of Afghans hidden in the villages and orchards on the east side of Sherpur had rushed out in one dense mob, and were filling the air with their shouts of "Allah-il-Allah." The roar surged forward as their line advanced, but it was answered by such a roll of musketry that it was drowned for the moment, and then merged into the general din which told us that our men with Martinis and Sniders were holding their own against the attacking force.' When the first attack thus graphically described was made the morning was still so dark and misty that the outlook from the trenches was restricted, and the order to the troops was to hold their fire till the assailants should be distinctly visible. The detachment of the 28th opened fire somewhat prematurely, and presently the Guides holding Behmaroo and the trenches on the slopes followed the example, and sweeping with their fire the terrain in front of them broke the force of the attack while its leaders were still several hundred yards away. Between the Hospital and the corner bastion the men of the 67th and 92d awaited with impassive discipline the word of permission to begin firing. From out the mist at length emerged dense masses of men, some of whom were brandishing swords and knives, while others loaded and fired while hurrying forward. The order to fire was not given until the leading ghazees were within eighty yards, and the mass of assailants not more distant than 200 yards. Heavily struck then by volley on volley, they recoiled but soon gathered courage to come on again; and for several hours there was sharp fighting, repeated efforts being made to carry the low eastern wall. So resolute were the Afghans that more than once they reached the abattis, but each time were driven back with heavy loss. About ten o'clock there was a lull and it seemed that the attacking force was owning the frustration of its attempts, but an hour later there was a partial recrudescence of the fighting and the assailants once more came on. The attack, however, was not pushed with much vigour and was soon beaten down, but the Afghans still maintained a threatening attitude and the fire from the defences was ineffectual to dislodge them. The General resolved to take their positions in flank, and with this intent sent out into the open through the gorge in the Behmaroo heights, four field guns escorted by a cavalry regiment. Bending to the right, the guns came into action on the right flank of the Afghans, and the counter-stroke had immediate effect. The enemy wavered and soon were in full retreat. The Kohistanee contingent, some 5000 strong, cut loose and marched away northward, with obvious recognition that the game was up. The fugitives were scourged with artillery and rifle fire, and Massy led out the cavalry, swept the plain, and drove the lingering Afghans from the slopes

110

KING'S ROYAL REGIMENT

of Siah Sung. The false attack on the southern face from the King's Garden and the Mahomed Shereef fort never made any head. Those positions were steadily shelled until late in the afternoon, when they were finally evacuated, and by nightfall all the villages and enclosures between Sherpur and Cabul were entirely deserted. Some of those had been destroyed by sappers from the garrison during the afternoon, in the course of which operation two gallant engineer officers, Captain Dundas and Lieutenant Nugent, were unfortunately killed by the premature explosion of a mine.

Mahomed Jan had been as good as his word; he had delivered his stroke against Sherpur, and that stroke had utterly failed. With its failure came promptly the collapse of the national rising. Before daybreak of the 24th the formidable combination which had included all the fighting elements of North-Eastern Afghanistan, and under whose banners it was believed that more than 100,000 armed men had mustered, was no more. Not only had it broken up; it had disappeared. Neither in the city, nor in the adjacent villages, nor on the surrounding heights, was a man to be seen. So hurried had been the Afghan dispersal that the dead lay unburied where they had fallen. His nine days on the defensive had cost General Roberts singularly little in casualties; his losses were eighteen killed and sixty-eight wounded. The enemy's loss from first to last of the rising was reckoned to be not under 3000.

On the 24th the cavalry rode far and fast in pursuit of the fugitives, but they overtook none, such haste had the fleeing Afghans made. On the same day Cabul and the Balla Hissar were reoccupied, and General Hills resumed his functions as military governor of the city. Cabul had the aspect of having undergone a sack at the hands of the enemy; the bazaars were broken up and deserted and the Hindoo and Kuzzilbash quarters had been relentlessly wrecked. Sir Frederick Roberts lost no time in despatching a column to the Kohistan to punish Meer Butcha by destroying that chief's forts and villages, and to ascertain whether the tribesmen of the district had dispersed to their homes. This was found to be the case, and the column returned after having been out five days. After making a few examples the General issued a proclamation of amnesty, excluding therefrom only five of the principal leaders and fomentors of the recent rising, and stipulating that the tribesmen should send representatives to Sherpur to receive explanations regarding the dispositions contemplated for the government of the country. This policy of conciliation bore good fruit; and a durbar was held on January 9th, 1880, at which were present about 200 sirdars, chiefs, and headmen from the Kohistan, Logur, and the Ghilzai country. Rewards were presented to those chiefs who had remained friendly; the General received the salaams of the assembled sirdars and then addressed them in a firm but conciliatory speech.

The country remained still in a disturbed state, but there was little likelihood of a second general rising. General Roberts was resolved, however, to be thoroughly prepared to cope with that contingency should it occur. Sherpur was encircled by a military road, and all cover and obstructions for the space of 1000 yards outside the enciente were swept away. Another road was constructed from Behmaroo village to the Siah Sung heights and yet another from the south-eastern gateway direct to the Balla Hissar, on both of which there were bridges across the Cabul river. Along the northern face of Cabul from Deh Afghan to the Balla Hissar, a road broad enough for guns was made, and another broad road cut through the lower Balla Hissar. Another military road was built through the Cabul gorge to the main Ghuznee and Bamian road in the Chardeh valley. Strong forts were built on the Asmai and Sher Derwaza heights and on the spur above the Balla Hissar, which, well garrisoned and supplied adequately with provisions, water, and ammunition, would enable Cabul as well as Sherpur to be held. The latter was greatly strengthened, the eastern point of the Behmaroo heights being converted into something like a regular fortress. Later, in March, when the Cabul force had increased to a strength of about 11,500 men and twenty-six guns, the command was formed into two divisions, of which the first remained under the Lieutenant-General, the second being commanded by Major-General John Ross. The line of communications was in charge of Major-General Bright, and Brigadier-General Hugh Gough was the cavalry commander in succession to Brigadier-General Massy. On the 2d of May, Sir Donald Stewart arriving at Cabul from Candahar, took over the chief command in North-Eastern Afghanistan from Sir Frederick Roberts. Sir Donald's march from Candahar, which was an eventful one, is dealt with in the next chapter.

Ahmed Khel

While Sir Frederick Roberts had been fighting hard in North-Eastern Afghanistan, Sir Donald Stewart had been experiencing comparative tranquillity in his Candahar command. As soon as the news reached him of the destruction of Cavagnari's mission he had promptly concentrated his troops, and so early as the third week of September (1879) he was in a position to carry out his orders to create a diversion in aid of Roberts' advance on Cabul by making a demonstration in the direction of Ghuznee and placing a garrison in Khelat-i-Ghilzai. No subsequent movements of importance were undertaken in Southern Afghanistan during the winter, and the province enjoyed almost unbroken quietude. In Herat, however, disturbance was rife. Ayoub Khan, the brother of Yakoub Khan, had returned from exile and made good his footing in Herat, of which formerly he had been conjoint governor with Yakoub. In December he began a hostile advance on Candahar, but a conflict broke out between the Cabul and Herat troops under his command, and he abandoned for the time his projected expedition.

In the end of March Sir Donald Stewart began the march toward Cabul which orders from India had prescribed. He left behind him in Candahar the Bombay division of his force under the command of Major-General Primrose, whose line of communication with the Indus valley was to be kept open by Phayre's brigade, and took with him on the northward march the Bengal division, consisting of two infantry brigades and a cavalry brigade. The first infantry brigade was commanded by Brigadier-General Barter, the second by Brigadier-General Hughes, and the cavalry brigade, which divisional headquarters accompanied, by Brigadier-General Palliser. Khelat-i-Ghilzai was reached on 6th April; the Bengal portion of its garrison joined the division and the advance was resumed on the following day. Until Shahjui, the limit of the Candahar province, the march was uneventful; but beyond that place extreme difficulties were experienced in procuring supplies, for the villages were found deserted and the inhabitants had carried off, destroyed, or hidden their stores of grain. The force was embarrassed by a horde of Hazaras, who swarmed in wild irregularity on its flanks, plundering and burning with great vindictiveness, eager to wreak vengeance on their Afghan foes. And it had another although more distant companionship, in the shape of several thousand hostile tribesmen and ghazees, whose fanaticism their moullas had been assiduously inciting, and who marched day by day parallel with the British right flank along the foothills at a distance of about eight miles. Their attitude was threatening but it was not thought wise to meddle with them, since their retreat over the hills could not well be cut off, and since the policy of non-interference would tend to encourage them to venture on a battle. The soundness of this reasoning was soon to be made manifest.

On the night of April 18th the division was encamped at Mushaki, about thirty miles south of Ghuznee. The spies that evening brought in the information that the enemy had resolved on fighting on the following morning, and that the position they intended to take up was the summit of a low spur of the Gul Koh mountain ridge, bounding on the west the valley followed by the road. This spur was said to project in a north-easterly direction toward the Ghuznee river, gradually sinking into the plain. During a great part of its length it flanked and overhung the road, but near where it merged into the plain the road passed over it by a low saddle at a point about six miles beyond Mushaki. At dawn of the 19th the column moved off, Palliser leading the advance, which Sir Donald Stewart accompanied, Hughes commanding the centre, Barter bringing up the rear and protecting the baggage. An hour later the enemy were visible in great strength about three miles in advance, presenting the aspect of a vast body formed up on the spur and on the saddle crossed by the road, and thus threatening Stewart at once in front and on both flanks. The British general at once made his dispositions. His guns were on the road in column of route. The three infantry regiments of Hughes' brigade came up to the left of and in line with the leading battery, the cavalry took ground on the plain on its right, and a reserve was formed consisting of an infantry regiment, two companies sappers and miners, and the General's escort of a troop and two companies. Orders were sent back to Barter to send forward without delay half the infantry of his brigade. In the formation described the force resumed its advance until within striking distance. Then the two batteries came into action on either side of the road; the horse-battery on the right, the flat ground to its right being covered by the 2d Punjaub Cavalry; the field-battery on the left. Sir Donald Stewart's proper front thus consisted of the field and horse-batteries with their supports, but since it was apparent that the greatest strength of the enemy was on the higher ground flanking his left, it behoved him to show a front in that direction also, and for this purpose he utilised Hughes' three infantry regiments, of which the 59th was on the right, the 2d Sikhs

DEATH OF MAJOR WIGRAM

in the centre, and the 3d Goorkhas on the left. Part of the reserve infantry was sent to make good the interval between the left of the artillery and the right of the infantry.

The guns had no sooner come into action than the enemy in great masses showed themselves on spur and saddle and plain, bent seemingly on an attempt to envelop the position held by the British. 'Suddenly,' writes Hensmen, 'a commotion was observed in the most advanced lines of the opposing army; the moullas could be seen haranguing the irregular host with frantic energy, the beating of the tom-toms was redoubled, and then as if by magic waves on waves of men—ghazees of the most desperate type—poured down upon the plain, and rushed upon General Stewart's force. The main body of the Afghan army remained upon the hill to watch the ghazees in their reckless onslaught, and take advantage of any success they might gain. The fanaticism of the 3000 or 4000 men who made this desperate charge has perhaps never been equalled; they had 500 or 600 yards to cover before they could come to close quarters, and yet they made nothing of the distance. Nearly all were well armed with tulwars, knives, and pistols. Some carried rifles and matchlocks, while a few—and those must have been resolute fanatics indeed—had simply pikes made of bayo-nets, or pieces of sharpened iron fastened on long shafts. Their attack broke with greatest violence on our flanks. On our left flank the 19th Bengal Lancers were still mov-ing into position when the ghazees rushed in among them. In an instant they were hidden in the cloud of dust and smoke, and then they galloped toward the right rear, and struck into the reserve in rear of the Lieutenant-General and his staff. All was confusion for a moment; the ammuni-tion mules were stampeded, and with the riderless horses of the lancers killed or wounded in the mêlée, dashed into the headquarter staff. The ghazees had continued their onward rush, and were engaged in hand-to-hand fighting with our infantry. Some of them penetrated to within twenty yards of the knoll on which the staff were watching the action, and so critical was the moment that Sir Donald Stewart and every man of his staff drew their swords and prepared for self-defence.' The hurried retirement of the lancers had left the left flank bare. It was turned by the fierce rush of the fanatics, who were actually in rear of the leftward infantry regiment and in the heart of the British position. The Goorkhas had been thrown into momentary confusion, but their colonel promptly formed them into rallying squares, whose fire mowed down the ghazees and arrested the headlong vehemence of their turning movement. But it was not the British left only which was temporarily compromised by the furious onslaught of the fanatics. Their enveloping charge broke down the defence of the weakly-manned interval between the left of the artillery and the right of the infantry. The detachments holding that interval were forced back, fighting hand-to-hand as the sheer weight of the assault compelled them to give ground; the 59th, in its effort to throw back its right to cover the interval and protect the guns, was thrown into confusion and gave ground; and the guns, their case shot exhausted and the Afghans within a few yards of their muzzles, had to be retired. The onslaught on the right front of the horse-battery was delivered with great determination, but was held at bay and finally crushed by the repeated charges of the 2d Punjaub cavalry.

Every man of the reserves was hurried into the fighting line; the soldiers were steadied by the energetic efforts of their officers and settled down to a steady and continuous fire from their breechloaders; the guns poured their shells into the hostile masses; and the fire of the forty-pounders on the left effectually arrested the attempt of the Afghan horse to move round that flank. The hard-fought combat lasted for an hour; at ten o'clock the 'cease fire' sounded, and the British victory was signal. The enemy was dispersing in full flight, and the cavalry was chasing the fugitives across the plain on the right. How reckless had been the whirlwind charges of the ghazees was evidenced by the extraordinary number of their dead whose corpses strewed the battlefield. In no previous conflict between our troops and the Afghans had the latter suffered nearly so heavily. More than 1000 dead were counted on the field, and many bodies were carried away; on a moderate computation their total loss must have been between 2000 and 3000, and that in an estimated strength of from 12,000 to 15,000. The casualties of the British force were seventeen killed and 124 wounded, of whom four died of their wounds. The injuries consisted almost wholly of sword slashes and knife stabs received in hand-to-hand encounters. The pursuit was soon recalled, but the Hazaras took up the chase with ardour and in the rancour of vengeance slew and spared not.

Sir Donald Stewart tarried on the field only long enough to bury his dead and have his wounded attended to; and soon after noon his force resumed its march. Ghuznee was reached on the 21st, where there was a halt of three days. It had been reported that the indomitable Mushk-i-Alum was raising the tribesmen of Zurmut and Shilgur to avenge the defeat of Ahmed Khel, and a cavalry reconnaissance made on the 22d had found a gathering of 2000 or 3000 men about the villages of Urzoo and Shalez, six miles south-east of Ghuznee. On the morning of the 23d a strong column commanded by Brigadier-General Palliser moved on the villages, which were found occupied in considerable force. They were too solidly built to be much injured by artillery fire, and the Afghans lay close in the shelter they afforded. Palliser hesitated to commit his infantry to an attack. Sir Donald Stewart having arrived, ordered the infantry to carry the villages without delay, and the affair was soon over, the tribesmen suffering severely from the rifle fire as they evacuated the villages, and later in the pursuit made by the cavalry and horse-artillery. On the following day the march toward Cabul was resumed.

On the 16th April Major-General Ross had been despatched from Cabul by Sir Frederick Roberts on the mission of joining hands with Stewart's division. On the 20th Ross opened heliographic communication with Sir Donald, and was informed of the latter's victory at Ahmed Khel. But the junction of the two forces was not accomplished until the 27th; and in the interval the force commanded by General Ross had received considerable annoyance at the hands of tribal levies gathered by local chiefs. The tribesmen interfered with the roadmaking operations of his sappers in the vicinity of Sheikabad, and some fighting occurred in very rugged country on the 23d. Trivial loss was experienced by his command, but the demonstrations of the tribesmen evinced with what inveterate determination, notwithstanding so many severe lessons, the Afghans persisted in their refusal to admit themselves conquered. Driven away with severe loss on the 25th, those indomitable hillmen and villagers were back again on the following morning on the overhanging ridges; nor were they dispersed by the 'resources of civilised warfare' until more of them had paid with their lives the penalty of their obstinate hostility. On the 28th, at Sheikabad, Sir Donald Stewart took leave of the division which he had led from Candahar, and proceeded to Cabul with General Ross' force to assume the chief command in North-Eastern Afghanistan. His division turned aside into the Logur valley, where it remained at until the final concentration about Cabul in anticipation of the evacuation. By the reinforcement brought by Stewart the Cabul field force was increased to a strength of about 18,000 men.

CHAPTER 7

The Ameer Abdurrahman

The occupation of Afghanistan by the British troops had been prolonged far beyond the period originally intended by the authorities. But the strain of that occupation was great, and although it had to be maintained until there should be found a ruler strong enough to hold his own after the evacuation, the decision was definitely arrived at to withdraw from the country before the setting in of another winter. Mr Lepel Griffin, a distinguished member of the political department of the Indian Civil Service, reached Cabul on 20th March, his mission being to further the selection and acceptance of a capable ruler to be left in possession. The task was no easy one. There was little promise in any of the Barakzai pretenders who were in Afghanistan, and in the address which Mr Griffin addressed in Durbar to a number of sirdars and chiefs in the middle of April, he preserved a tone at once haughty and enigmatical. One thing he definitely announced, the Viceroy's decision that Yakoub Khan was not to return to Afghanistan. The State was to be dismembered. As to the future of Herat the speaker made no allusion; but the province of Candahar was to be separated from Cabul and placed under an independent Barakzai prince. No decision could for the present be given in regard to the choice of an Ameer to rule over Cabul. The Government desired to nominate an Ameer strong enough to govern his people and steadfast in his friendship to the British; if those qualifications could be secured the Government was willing and anxious to recognise the wish of the Afghan people, and nominate an Ameer of their choice.

But in effect the choice, so far as the English were concerned, had been already virtually made. On the 14th of March Lord Lytton had telegraphed to the Secretary of State advocating the 'early public recognition of Abdurrahman as legitimate heir of Dost Mahomed, and the despatch of a deputation of sirdars, with British concurrence, to offer him the throne, as sole means of saving the country from anarchy'; and the Minister had promptly replied authorising the nomination of Abdurrahman, should he be found 'acceptable to the country and would be contented with Northern Afghanistan.' Abdurrahman had known strange vicissitudes. He was the eldest grandson of the old Dost; his father was Afzul Khan, the elder brother of Shere Ali. After the death of the Dost he had been an exile in Bokhara, but he returned to Balkh, of which province his father had been Governor until removed by Shere Ali, made good his footing there, and having done so advanced on Cabul, taking advantage of Shere Ali's absence at Candahar. The capital opened its gates to him in March 1866; he fought a successful battle with Shere Ali at Sheikabad, occupied Ghuznee, and proclaimed his father Ameer. Those were triumphs, but soon the wheel came round full circle. Afzul had but a short life as Ameer, and Abdurrahman had to retire to Afghan Turkestan. Yakoub, then full of vigour and enterprise, defeated him at Bamian and restored his father Shere Ali to the throne in the winter of 1868. Abdurrahman then once more found himself an exile. In 1870, after much wandering, he reached Tashkend, where General Kaufmann gave him permission to reside, and obtained for him from the Czar a pension of 25,000 roubles per annum. Petrosvky, a Russian writer who professed to be intimate with him during his period of exile, wrote of him that, 'To get square some day with the English and Shere Ali was Abdurrahman's most cherished thought, his dominant, never-failing passion.' His hatred of Shere Ali, his family, and supporters, was intelligible and natural enough, but why he should have entertained a bitter grudge against the English is not very apparent; and there has been no overt manifestation of its existence since he became Ameer. To Mr Eugene Schuyler, who had an interview with him at Tashkend, he expressed his conviction that with £50,000 wherewith to raise and equip an army he could attain his legitimate position as Ameer of Afghanistan. Resolutely bent on an effort to accomplish this purpose, he was living penuriously and saving the greater part of his pension, and he hinted that he might have Russian assistance in the prosecution of his endeavour. The selection of a man of such antecedents and associations as the ruler of a 'buffer' state in friendly relations with British India was perhaps the greatest leap in the dark on record. Abdurrahman came straight from the position of a Russian pensionary; in moving on Afghanistan he obeyed Russian instructions; his Tashkend patrons had furnished him with a modest equipment of arms and money, the value of which he undertook to repay if successful. It is of course possible that those functionaries of a notoriously simple and ingenuous government started and equipped him in pure friendly good nature, although they had previously consistently deterred him. But there was not a circumstance in connection with Abdurrahman that was not suspicious. Three distinct hypotheses seem to present themselves in relation to this selection as our nominee; that Lord Lytton had extraordinary, almost indeed preternatural foresight and sagacity; that he was extremely fortunate in his leap in the dark; that he desired to bring to the naked reductio ad absurdum the 'buffer state' policy. When Abdurrahman began his movement is uncertain. So early as the middle of January it was reported at Sherpur that he had left Tashkend, and was probably already on the Afghan side of the Oxus. In a letter of February 17th Mr Hensman speaks of him as being in Badakshan, where his wife's kinsmen were in power, and describes him as having a following of 2000 or 3000 Turcoman horsemen and possessed according to native report of twelve lakhs of rupees. On the 17th of March Lord Lytton telegraphed to the Secretary of State that he was in possession of 'authentic intelligence that the Sirdar was in Afghan Turkestan, having lately arrived there from Badakshan.'

It was regarded of urgent importance to ascertain definitely the disposition of Abdurrahman, and whether he was disposed to throw in his lot with the British Government, and accept the position of its nominee in Northern Afghanistan. The agent selected by Mr Griffin to open preliminary negotiations was a certain Mohamed Surwar, Ghilzai, who had been all his life in the confidential service of the Sirdar's family. Surwar was the bearer of a formal and colourless letter by way simply of authentication; but he also carried full and explicit verbal instructions. He was directed to inform the Sirdar that since he had entered Afghan Turkestan and occupied places there by force of arms, it was essential for him to declare with what object he had come, and whether actuated by friendly or hostile feelings toward the British Government, which for its part had no ill-feeling toward him because of his long residence within the Russian Empire and his notoriously close relations with that power. That the British Government was able to benefit him very largely in comparison with that of Russia; and that wisdom and self interest alike suggested that he should at once open a friendly correspondence with the British officers in Cabul. That his opportunity was now come, and that the British Government was disposed to treat him with every consideration and to consider most favourably any representations he might make. It had no intention of annexing the country, and only desired to see a strong and friendly chief established at Cabul; and that consequently the present communication was made solely in Abdurrahman's own interest, and not in that of the British Government. He was desired to send a reply by Surwar, and later to repair to Cabul, where he should be honourably received.

Surwar returned to Cabul on 21st April, bringing a reply from Abdurrahman to Mr Griffin's letter. The tone of the reply was friendly enough, but somewhat indefinite. In conversation with Surwar as reported by the latter, Abdurrahman was perfectly frank as to his relations with the Russians, and his sentiments in regard to them. It had been reported that he had made his escape clandestinely from Tashkend. Had he cared to stand well with us at the expense of truth, it would have been his cue to disclaim all authority or assistance from the Russian Government, to confirm the current story of his escape, and to profess his anxiety to cultivate friendly relations with the British in a spirit of opposition to the power in whose territory he had lived so long virtually as a prisoner. But neither in writing nor in conversation did he make any concealment of his friendliness toward the Russians, a feeling which he clearly regarded as nowise incompatible with friendly relations with the British Government. 'If,' said he to Surwar, 'the English will in sincerity befriend me, I have no wish to hide anything from them'; and he went on to tell how the Russians had forbidden him for years to make any effort to interfere in Afghan affairs. This prohibition stood until information reached Tashkend of the deportation of Yakoub Khan to India. Then it was that General Kaufmann's representative said to him: 'You have always been anxious to return to your country; the English have removed Yakoub Khan; the opportunity is favourable; if you wish you are at liberty to go.' The Russians, continued Abdurrahman, pressed him most strongly to set out on the enterprise which lay before him. They lent him 33,000 rupees, and arms, ammunition, and supplies; he was bound to the Russians by no path or promise, but simply by feelings of gratitude. 'I should never like,' said he, 'to be obliged to fight them. I have eaten their salt, and was for twelve years dependent on their hospitality.'

Surwar reported Abdurrahman as in fine health and possessed of great energy. He had with him a force of about 3000 men, consisting of four infantry and two cavalry regiments, with twelve guns and some irregulars. He professed his readiness, in preference to conducting negotiations through agents, to go himself to Charikar in the Kohistan with an escort, and there discuss matters with the English officers in person. Surwar testified that the Sirdar had with him in Turkestan no Russian or Russian agent, and this was confirmed through other sources. He had sent forward to ascertain which was the easiest pass across the Hindoo Koosh, but meanwhile he was to remain at Kondooz until he should hear again from Mr Griffin.

While the wary Sirdar waited on events beyond the Hindoo Koosh he was sending letters to the leading chiefs of the Kohistan and the Cabul province, desiring them to be ready to support his cause. That he had an influential party was made clear at a durbar held by Mr Griffin on April 21st, when a considerable gathering of important chiefs united in the request that Abdurrahman's claim to the Ameership should be favourably regarded by the British authorities. In pursuance of the negotiations a mission consisting of three Afghan gentlemen, two of whom belonged to Mr Griffin's political staff, left Cabul on May 2nd carrying to Abdurrahman a letter from Mr Griffin intimating that it had been decided to withdraw the British army from Afghanistan in the course of a few months, and that the British authorities desired to leave the rulership in capable and friendly hands; that they were therefore willing to transfer the Government to him, recognise him as the head of the State, and afford him facilities and even support in reorganising the Government and establishing himself in the sovereignty. The mission found the attitude of Abdurrahman scarcely so satisfactory as had been reported by Surwar, and its members were virtual prisoners, their tents surrounded by sentries. Abdurrahman's explanation of this rigour of isolation was that he could not otherwise ensure the safety of the envoys; but another construction conveyed to them was that they were kept prisoners that they might not, by mixing with the people, learn of the presence on the right bank of the Oxus of a Russian officer with whom Abdurrahman was said to be in constant communication and on whose advice he acted. Their belief was that Abdurrahman was entirely under Russian influence; that Mr Griffin's letter after it had been read in Durbar in the camp was immediately despatched across the Oxus by means of mounted relays; and that Russian instructions as to a reply had not been received when they left Turkestan to return to Cabul. They expressed their belief that the Sirdar would not accept from British hands Cabul shorn of Candahar. They had urged him to repeat in the letter they were to carry back to Cabul the expression of his willingness to meet the British representative at Charikar which had been contained in his letter sent by Surwar; but he demurred to committing himself even to this slight extent. The letter which he sent by way of reply to the weighty communication Mr Griffin had addressed to him on the part of the Government of India that official characterised as 'frivolous and empty, and only saved by its special courtesy of tone from being an impertinence.'

An Afghan who had sat at Kaufmann's feet, Abdurrahman was not wholly a guileless man; and the truth probably was that he mistrusted the Greeks of Simla and the gifts they tendered him with so lavish protestation that they were entirely for his own interest. There was very little finesse about the importunity of the British that he should constitute himself their bridge of extrication, so that they might get out of Afghanistan without the dangers and discredit of leaving chaos behind them. But Abdurrahman had come to know himself strong enough to reduce to order that legacy of chaos if it should be left; and in view of his future relations with his fellow Afghans he was not solicitous to be beholden to the foreigners to any embarrassing extent. He knew, too, the wisdom of 'masterly inactivity' in delicate conditions. And, again, he had no confidence in our pledges. On the 4th of August, the day after the meeting between him and Mr Griffin at Zimma, the latter wrote: 'They (Abdurrahman and his advisers) feared greatly our intention was to rid ourselves of a formidable opponent, and dreaded that if he had come straight into Cabul he would have been arrested, and deported to India.'

A Liberal Government was now in office in England, and was urgent for the speedy evacuation of Afghanistan. Lord Lytton had resigned and had been succeeded as Viceroy by the Marquis of Ripon. Lieutenant-General Sir Donald Stewart was in chief command at Cabul. A great number of letters from Abdurrahman to chiefs and influential persons throughout Afghanistan were being intercepted, the tone of which was considered objectionable. He was reported to be in close correspondence with Mahomed Jan, who had

never ceased to be our bitter enemy. The fact that negotiations were in progress between the British Government
and Abdurrahman had become matter of general knowl-
edge throughout the country, and was occasioning disqui-
etude and excitement. So clear were held the evidences of
what was termed Abdurrahman's bad faith, but was probably a combination of genuine mistrust, astute passivity, and
shrewd playing for his own hand, that it became a serious
question with the Indian Government on the arrival of the
new Viceroy, whether it was good policy to have anything
more to do with him. It was resolved that before breaking
off intercourse the suggestion of Sir Donald Stewart and
Mr Griffin should be adopted, that a peremptory although
still friendly letter, demanding a definite acceptance or refusal of the proffers made, within four days after the receipt,
should be sent to Abdurrahman, with a detailed explanation of the arrangements into which we were prepared to
enter with regard to him and the future of Afghanistan. A
letter was forwarded from Cabul on 14th June, in which Mr
Griffin informed the Sirdar that since the British Government admitted no right of interference by foreign powers
in Afghanistan, it was plain that the Cabul ruler could have
no political relations with any foreign power except the
English; and if any foreign power should attempt to interfere in Afghanistan, and if such interference should lead to
unprovoked aggression on the Cabul ruler, then the British
Government would be prepared to aid him, if necessary, to
repel it. As regarded limits of the territory, the latter stated
that the whole province of Candahar had been placed under a separate ruler, except Sibi and Pisheen, which were
retained in British possession. Consequently the British
Government was unable to enter into any negotiations on
those points, or in respect to arrangements in regard to the
north-western frontier which were settled by the treaty of

Gundamuk. Subject to those reservations, the British Government was willing that Abdurrahman should establish over Afghanistan—including Herat when he should have conquered it—as complete and extensive authority as was swayed by any previous Ameer. The British Government would exercise no interference in the internal government of those territories nor would it demand the acceptance of an English Resident anywhere within Afghanistan, although for convenience of ordinary friendly intercourse it might be agreed upon that a Mahommedan Agent of the British Government should be stationed at Cabul.

Abdurrahman's reply to this communication was vague and evasive, and was regarded by Sir Donald Stewart and Mr Griffin as so unsatisfactory that they represented to the Government of India, not for the first time, their conviction of the danger of trusting Abdurrahman, the imprudence of delaying immediate action, and the necessity of breaking off with him and adopting other means of establishing a government in Cabul before the impending evacuation. Lord Ripon, however, considered that 'as matters stood an arrangement with Abdurrahman offered the most advisable solution, while he doubted whether it would not be found very difficult to enter into any alternative arrangement.' His Excellency's decision was justified by the event. Meanwhile, indeed, Abdurrahman had started on June 28th for the Kohistan. He crossed the Hindoo Koosh and arrived on July 20th at Charikar, where he was welcomed by a deputation of leading chiefs, while the old Mushk-i-Alum, who for some time, thanks to Mr Griffin's influence, had been working in the interests of peace, intimated on behalf of a number of chiefs assembled in Maidan that they were ready to accept as Ameer the nominee of the British Government.

So propitious seemed the situation that it was considered

the time had come for formally acknowledging Abdurrahman as the new Ameer, and also for fixing approximately the date of the evacuation of Cabul by the British troops. The ceremony of recognition was enacted in a great durbar tent within the Sherpur cantonment on the afternoon of July 22d. The absence of Abdurrahman, and the notorious cause of that absence, detracted from the intrinsic dignity of the occasion so far as concerned the British participation in it; nor was the balance restored by the presence of three members of his suite whom he had delegated to represent him. A large number of sirdars, chiefs, and maliks were present, some of whom had fought stoutly against us in December. Sir Donald Stewart, who presided, explained to the assembled Afghans that their presence and that of the officers of the British force had been called for in order that the public recognition by the British Government of the Sirdar Abdurrahman Khan as Ameer of Cabul should be made known with as much honour as possible. Then Mr Griffin addressed in Persian a short speech to the 'sirdars, chiefs, and gentlemen' who constituted his audience. Having announced the recognition of Abdurrahman by 'the Viceroy of India and the Government of Her Most Gracious Majesty the Queen Empress,' he proceeded: 'It is to the Government a source of satisfaction that the tribes and chiefs have preferred as Ameer a distinguished member of the Barakzai family, who is a renowned soldier, wise, and experienced. His sentiments towards the British Government are most friendly; and so long as his rule shows that he is animated by these sentiments, he cannot fail to receive the support of the British Government.' Mr Griffin then intimated that the British armies would shortly withdraw from Afghanistan; and in his formal farewell there was a certain appropriate dignity, and a well-earned tribute to the conduct of our soldiers during their service within the Afghan borders. 'We trust and firmly believe,' said Mr Griffin, 'that your remembrance of the English will not be unkindly. We have fought you in the field whenever you have opposed us; but your religion has in no way been interfered with; the honour of your women has been respected, and every one has been secure in possession of his property. Whatever has been necessary for the support of the army has been liberally paid for. Since I came to Cabul I have been in daily intercourse with you, but I have never heard an Afghan make a complaint of the conduct of any soldier, English or native, belonging to Her Majesty's army.' The durbar was closed by an earnest appeal by Sir Donald Stewart to all the sirdars and chiefs that they should put aside their private feuds and unite to support the new Ameer.

On August 3rd Abdurrahman and Mr Griffin at length met, about sixteen miles north of Cabul. His adherents were still full of excitement and suspicion; but the Ameer himself was calm, cheerful, and dignified. The conference between him and Mr Griffin lasted for three hours and was renewed on the following day. 'He appeared,' wrote Mr Griffin, 'animated by a sincere desire to be on cordial terms with the British Government, and although his expectations were larger than the Government was prepared to satisfy, yet he did not press them with any discourteous insistence, and the result of the interview may be considered on the whole to be highly satisfactory.' The tidings of the Maiwand disaster had reached Sherpur by telegraph, and the Ameer was informed that a necessity might occur for marching a force from Cabul to Candahar. His reply was that the tribes might be hostile, but that if no long halts were made by the way he would have no objections to such a march. In this he showed his astuteness, since the defeat of Ayoub Khan by a British army would obviously save him a contest. So willing to be of service on this matter was he that when

E Battery Escaping

the march was decided on he sent influential persons of his party in advance to arrange with the local maliks to have supplies collected for the column. The arrangements made with him were that he was to fall heir to the thirty guns of Shere Ali's manufacture which the out-marching army was to leave in Sherpur, and was to receive 19½ lakhs of rupees (£190,500); ten lakhs of which were given as an earnest of British friendship, and the balance was money belonging to the Afghan State, which had gone into the commissariat chest and was now restored. At the Ameer's earnest and repeated request the forts which had been built around Cabul by the British army, were not destroyed as had been intended, but were handed over intact to the new Ameer.

It seemed that Sir Donald Stewart, who was to evacuate Sherpur on the 11th August, would leave Cabul without seeing Abdurrahman. But at the last moment Mr Griffin succeeded in arranging an interview. It was held early in the morning of the evacuation, in a tent just outside the Sherpur cantonment, was quite public, and lasted only for quarter of an hour. Abdurrahman was frank and cordial. He said that his heart was full of gratitude to the British, and desired that his best thanks should be communicated to the Viceroy. At the close of the interview he shook hands with all 'who cared to wish him good-bye and good luck,' and sent his principal officer to accompany the General on his first day's march, which began immediately after the parting with Abdurrahman. Sir Donald Stewart's march down the passes was accomplished without incident, quite unmolested by the tribes. Small garrisons were temporarily left in the Khyber posts, and the war-worn regiments were dispersed through the stations of North-Western India.

CHAPTER 8

Maiwand and the Great March

When in the early spring of 1880 Sir Donald Stewart quitted Candahar with the Bengal division of his force, he left there the Bombay division, to the command of which General Primrose acceded, General Phayre assuming charge of the communications. The province during the early summer was fairly quiet, but it was known that Ayoub Khan was making hostile preparations at Herat, although the reports as to his intentions and movements were long uncertain and conflicting. Shere Ali Khan, who had been Governor of Candahar during Stewart's residence there, had been nominated hereditary ruler of the province with the title of 'Wali,' when it was determined to separate Candahar from North-Eastern Afghanistan. On June 21st the Wali, who had some days earlier crossed the Helmund and occupied Girishk with his troops, reported that Ayoub was actually on the march toward the Candahar frontier, and asked for the support of a British brigade to enable him to cope with the hostile advance. There was reason to believe that the Wali's troops were disaffected, and that he was in no condition to meet Ayoub's army with any likelihood of success. After Stewart's departure the strength of the British forces at Candahar was dangerously low—only 4700 of all ranks; but it was important to thwart Ayoub's offensive movement, and a brigade consisting of a troop of horse-artillery, six companies of the 66th, two Bombay native infantry regiments, and 500 native troopers, in all about 2300 strong, under the command of Brigadier-General Burrows, reached the left bank of the Helmund on July 11th. On the 13th the Wali's infantry, 2000 strong, mutinied en masse and marched away up the right bank of the river, taking with them a battery of smooth bore guns, a present to Shere Ali Khan from the British Government. His cavalry did not behave quite so badly, but, not to go into detail, his army no longer existed, and Burrows' brigade was the only force in the field to resist the advance of Ayoub Khan, whose regular troops were reported to number 4000 cavalry, and from 4000 to 5000 infantry exclusive of the 2000 deserters from the Wali, with thirty guns and an irregular force of uncertain strength.

Burrows promptly recaptured from the Wali's infantry the battery they were carrying off, and punished them severely. The mutineers had removed or destroyed the supplies which the Wali had accumulated for the use of the brigade, and General Burrows therefore could no longer remain in the vicinity of Girishk. The Helmund owing to the dry season was passable everywhere, so that nothing was to be gained by watching the fords. It was determined to fall back to Khushk-i-Nakhud, a point distant thirty miles from Girishk and forty-five from Candahar, where several roads from the Helmund converged and where supplies were plentiful. At and near Khushk-i-Nakhud the brigade remained from the 16th until the morning of the 27th July. While waiting and watching there a despatch from army headquarters at Simla was communicated to General Burrows from Candahar, authorising him to attack Ayoub if he thought himself strong enough to beat him, and informing him that it was considered of the greatest political importance that the force from Herat should be dispersed and prevented from moving on toward Ghuznee. Spies brought in news that Ayoub had reached Girishk, and was distributing his force along the right bank between that place and Hydrabad. Cavalry patrols failed to find the enemy until the 21st, when a detachment was encountered in the village of Sangbur on the northern road about midway between the Helmund and Khushk-i-Nakhud. Next day that village was found more strongly occupied, and on the 23rd a reconnaissance in force came upon a body of Ayoub's horsemen in the plain below the Garmao hills, about midway between Sangbur and Maiwand.

Those discoveries were tolerably clear indications of Ayoub's intention to turn Burrows' position by moving along the northern road to Maiwand and thence pressing on through the Maiwand pass, until at Singiri Ayoub's army should have interposed itself between the brigade and Candahar. There was certainly nothing impossible in such an endeavour, since Maiwand is nearer Candahar than is Khushk-i-Nakhud. Why, in the face of the information at his disposal and of the precautions enjoined on him to hinder Ayoub from slipping by him toward Ghuznee through Maiwand and up the Khakrez valley, General Burrows should have remained so long at Khushk-i-Nakhud, is not intelligible. He was stirred at length on the afternoon of the 26th, by the report that 2000 of Yakoub's cavalry and a large body of his ghazees were in possession of Garmao and Maiwand, and were to be promptly followed by Ayoub himself with the main body of his army, his reported intention being to push on through the Maiwand pass and reach the Urgundab valley in rear of the British brigade. Later in the day Colonel St John, the political officer, reported to General Burrows the intelligence which had reached him that the whole of Ayoub's army was at Sangbur; but credence was not given to the information.

The somewhat tardy resolution was taken to march to Maiwand on the morning of the 27th. There was the expectation that the brigade would arrive at that place before the enemy should have occupied it in force, and this point made good there might be the opportunity to drive out of Garmao the body of Yakoub's cavalry reported in possession there. There was a further reason why Maiwand should be promptly occupied; the brigade had been obtaining its supplies from that village, and there was still a quantity of grain in its vicinity to lose which would be unfortunate. The brigade, now 2600 strong, struck camp on the morning of the 27th. The march to Maiwand was twelve miles long, and an earlier start than 6.30 would have been judicious. The soldiers marched fast, but halts from time to time were necessary to allow the baggage to come up; the hostile state of the country did not admit of anything being left behind and the column was encumbered by a great quantity of stores and baggage. At Karezah, eight miles from Khushk-i-Nakhud and four miles south-west of Maiwand, information was brought in that the whole of Yakoub's army was close by on the left front of the brigade, and marching toward Maiwand. The spies had previously proved themselves so untrustworthy that small heed was taken of this report; but a little later a cavalry reconnaissance found large bodies of cavalry moving in the direction indicated and inclining away toward Garmao as the brigade advanced. A thick haze made it impossible to discern what force, if any, was being covered by the cavalry. About ten A.M. the advance guard occupied the village of Mundabad, about three miles south-west of Maiwand. West of Mundabad, close to the village, was a broad and deep ravine running north and south. Beyond this ravine was a wide expanse of level and partially cultivated plain across which, almost entirely concealed by the haze, Ayoub's army was marching eastward toward Maiwand village, which covers the western entrance to the pass of the same name. If General Burrows' eye could have penetrated that haze, probably he would have considered it prudent to take up a defensive position, for which Mundabad presented many advantages. But he was firm in the conviction that the enemy's guns were not up, notwithstanding the reports of spies to the contrary; he believed that a favourable opportunity presented itself for taking the initiative, and he resolved to attack with all possible speed.

Lieutenant Maclaine of the Horse-Artillery, a gallant young officer who was soon to meet a melancholy fate, precipitated events in a somewhat reckless fashion. With the two guns he commanded he crossed the ravine, galloped across the plain, and opened fire on a body of Afghan cavalry which had just come within view. General Nuttall, commanding the cavalry and horse-artillery, failing to recall Maclaine, sent forward in support of him the four remaining guns of the battery. Those approached to within 800 yards of the two advanced pieces, and Maclaine was directed to fall back upon the battery pending the arrival of the brigade, which General Burrows was now sending forward. It crossed the ravine near Mundabad, advanced on the plain about a mile in a north-westerly direction, and then formed up. There were several changes in the dispositions; when the engagement became warm about noon the formation was as follows:—The 66th foot was on the right, its right flank thrown back to check an attempt made to turn it by a rush of ghazees springing out of the ravine in the British front; on the left of the 66th were four companies of Jacob's Rifles (30th Native Infantry) and a company of sappers, the centre was occupied by the horse-artillery and smooth bore guns, of which latter, however, two had been moved to the right flank; on the left of the guns were the its Grenadiers somewhat refused, and on the extreme left two companies of Jacob's Rifles. The cavalry was in the rear, engaged in efforts to prevent the Afghans from taking the British infantry in reverse. The position was radically faulty, and indeed invited disaster. Both flanks were *en l'air* in face of an enemy of greatly superior strength; almost from the first every rifle was in the fighting line, and the sole reserve consisted of the two cavalry regiments. The baggage had followed the brigade across the ravine and was halted about 1000 yards in rear of the right, inadequately guarded by cavalry detachments.

For half-an-hour no reply was made to the British shell fire, and an offensive movement at this time might have resulted in success. But presently battery after battery was brought into action by the Afghans, until half-an-hour after noon the fire of thirty guns was concentrated on the brigade. Under cover of this artillery fire the ghazees from the ravine charged forward to within 500 yards of the 66th, but the rifle fire of the British regiment drove them back with heavy loss, and they recoiled as far as the ravine, whence they maintained a desultory fire. The enemy's artillery fire was well sustained and effective; the infantry found some protection from it in lying down, but the artillery and cavalry remained exposed and suffered severely. An artillery duel was maintained for two hours, greatly to the disadvantage of the brigade, which had but twelve guns in action against thirty well-served Afghan pieces. The prostrate infantry had escaped serious punishment, but by two P.M. the cavalry had lost fourteen per cent, of the men in the front line, and 149 horses; the Afghan horsemen had turned both flanks and the brigade was all but surrounded, while a separate attack was being made on the baggage. Heat and want of water were telling heavily on the sepoys, who were further demoralised by the Afghan artillery fire.

A little later the smooth bore guns had to be with-drawn for want of ammunition. This was the signal for a general advance of the Afghans. Their guns were pushed forward with great boldness; their cavalry streamed round the British left; in the right rear were masses of mounted and dismounted irregulars who had seized the villages on the British line of retreat. Swarms of ghazees soon showed themselves threatening the centre and left; those in front of the 66th were still held in check by the steady volleys fired by that regiment. At sight of the ghazees, and cowed by the heavy artillery fire and the loss of their officers, the two companies of Jacob's Rifles on the left suddenly fell into confusion, and broke into the ranks of the Grenadiers. That regiment had behaved well but it caught the infection of demoralisation, the whole left collapsed, and the sepoys in utter panic, surrounded by and intermingled with the ghazees, rolled in a great wave upon the right. The artillery-men and sappers made a gallant stand, fighting the ghazees hand-to-hand with handspikes and rammers, while the guns poured canister into the advancing masses. Slade re-luctantly limbered up and took his four guns out of action; Maclaine remained in action until the ghazees were at the muzzles of his two guns, which fell into the enemy's hands. The torrent of mingled sepoys and ghazees broke in upon the 66th, and overwhelmed that regiment. The slaughter of the sepoys was appalling—so utterly cowed were they that they scarcely attempted to defend themselves, and al-lowed themselves without resistance to be dragged out of the ranks and killed. A cavalry charge was ordered in the direction of the captured guns, but it failed and the troopers retired in disorder. The infantry, assailed by hordes of fierce and triumphant ghazees, staggered away to the right, the 66th alone maintaining any show of formation, until the ravine was crossed, when the broken remnants of the sepoy regiments took to flight toward the east and the General's efforts to rally them were wholly unavailing. The 66th with some of the sappers and grenadiers, made a gallant stand round its colours in an enclosure near the village of Khig. There Colonel Galbraith and several of his officers were killed, and the little body of brave men becoming out-flanked, continued its retreat, making stand after stand until most were slain. The Afghans pursued for about four miles, but were checked by a detachment of rallied cavalry, and desisted. The fugitives, forming with wounded and baggage a straggling column upwards of six miles long, crossed the waterless desert sixteen miles wide, to Hanz-i-Madat, which was reached about midnight and where water was found. From Asu Khan, where cultivation began, to Kokoran near Candahar, the retreat was harassed by armed villagers and the troops had to fight more or less all the way. Officers and men were killed, Lieutenant Maclaine was taken prisoner, and five of the smooth bore guns had to be abandoned be-cause of the exhaustion of the teams. About midday of the 28th the broken remnants of the brigade reached Canda-har. When the casualties were ascertained it became evident how disastrous to the British arms had been the combat of Maiwand. Out of a total of 2476 engaged no fewer than 964 were killed. The wounded numbered 167; 331 follow-ers and 201 horses were killed and seven followers and six-ty-eight horses wounded. Since Chillianwallah the British arms in Asia had not suffered loss so severe.

The spirit of the Candahar force suffered materially from the Maiwand disaster, and it was held that there was no al-ternative but to accept the humiliation of a siege within the fortified city. The cantonments were abandoned, the whole force was withdrawn into Candahar, and was de-tailed for duty on the city walls. The effective garrison on the night of the 28th numbered 4360, including the survivors of the Maiwand brigade. So alert were the Afghans that a cavalry reconnaissance made on the morning of the 29th, found the cantonments plundered and partly burned and the vicinity of Candahar swarming with armed men. The whole Afghan population amounting to about 12,000 persons, were compelled to leave the city, and then the work of placing it in a state of defence was energetically undertaken. Buildings and enclosures affording cover too close to the enciente were razed, communication along the walls was opened up, and gun platforms were constructed in the more commanding positions. The walls were both high and thick, but they were considerably dilapidated and there were gaps and breaks in the bastions and parapet. The weak places as well as the gates were fronted with abattis, the defects were made good with sandbags, and wire entanglements and other obstructions were laid down outside the walls. While this work was in progress the covering parties were in daily collision with the enemy, and occasional sharp skirmishes occurred.

On the 8th August Ayoub opened fire on the citadel from Picquet hill, an elevation north-westward of the city, and a few days later he brought guns into action from the villages of Deh Khoja and Deh Khati on the east and south. This fire, steadily maintained though it was day after day, had little effect, and the return fire gave good results. It was not easy to invest the city since on the west and north there was no cover for the besiegers, but in Deh Khoja on the east there was ample protection for batteries, and the ground on the south-west was very favourable. Its advantages were improved so skilfully that it was at one time believed there was a European engineer in Ayoub's camp. Deh Khoja was inconveniently near the Cabul gate, and was always full of men. So menacing was the attitude of the Afghans that a sortie was resolved on against the village, which was conducted with resolution but resulted in utter failure. The attempt was made on the morning of the 16th. The cavalry went out to hinder reinforcements from entering the village from the eastward. An infantry force 800 strong commanded by Brigadier-General Brooke and divided into three parties, moved out later covered by a heavy artillery fire from the city walls. The village was reached, but was so full of enemies in occupation of the fortress-like houses that it was found untenable, and the three detachments extricated themselves separately. In the course of the retirement General Brooke and Captain Cruickshank were killed. The casualties were very heavy; 106 were killed and 117 were wounded.

The tidings of the Maiwand disaster reached Cabul on the 29th July by telegram from Simla. The intention of the military authorities had already been intimated that the Cabul force should evacuate Afghanistan in two separate bodies and by two distinct routes. Sir Donald Stewart was to march one portion by the Khyber route; the other under Sir Frederick Roberts was to retire by the Kuram valley, which Watson's division had been garrisoning since Roberts had crossed the Shutargurdan in September 1879. But the Maiwand news interfered with those arrangements. Stewart and Roberts concurred in the necessity of retrieving the Maiwand disaster by the despatch of a division from Cabul. Roberts promptly offered to lead that division, and as promptly the offer was accepted by Stewart. By arrangement with the latter Roberts telegraphed to Simla urging that a force should be despatched from Cabul without delay; and recognising that the authorities might hesitate to send on this errand troops already under orders to return to India, he took it on himself to guarantee that none of the soldiers would demur, providing he was authorised to give the assurance that after the work in the field was over they would not be detained in garrison at Candahar. The Viceroy's sanction came on the 3d August. The constitution and equipment of the force were entrusted to the two generals; and in reply to questions His Excellency was informed that Roberts would march on the 8th and expected to reach Candahar on 2d September. Sir Donald Stewart gave his junior full freedom to select the troops to accompany him, and placed at his disposal the entire resources of the army in transport and equipment. It cannot truly be said that it was the elite of the Cabul field force which constituted the column led by Roberts in his famous march to Candahar. Of the native infantry regiments of his own original force which he had mustered eleven months previously in the Kuram only two followed him to Candahar, the 5th Goorkhas and 23d Pioneers, and the second mountain battery adhered to him staunchly, Of his original white troops the 9th Lancers, as ever, were ready for the march. His senior infantry regiment, the 67th, would fain have gone, but the good old corps was weak from casualties and sickness, and the gallant Knowles denied himself in the interests of his men. The two Highland regiments, the 72d and 92d, had done an infinity of fighting and marching, but both had received strong drafts, were in fine condition, and were not to be hindered from following the chief whom, though not of their northern blood, the stalwart sons of the mist swore by as one man.

Sir Frederick Roberts had already represented that it would be impolitic to require the native regiments to remain absent from India and their homes for a longer period than two years. In the case of many of the regiments that term was closely approached, and the men after prolonged absence and arduous toil needed rest and were longing to rejoin their families. 'It was not,' in the words of General Chapman, 'with eager desire that the honour of marching to Candahar was sought for, and some commanding officers of experience judged rightly the tempers of their men when they represented for the General's consideration the claims of the regiments they commanded to be relieved as soon as possible from field service....The enthusiasm which carried Sir Frederick Roberts' force with exceptional rapidity to Candahar was an after-growth evolved by the enterprise itself, and came as a response to the unfailing spirit which animated the leader himself.' The constitution of the force was made known by the general orders published on 3d August. It consisted of three batteries of artillery commanded by Colonel Alured Johnson; of a cavalry brigade of four regiments commanded by Brigadier-General Hugh Gough; and of an infantry division of three brigades commanded by Major-General John Ross. The first brigade was commanded by Brigadier-General Herbert Macpherson, the second by Brigadier-General T. D. Baker, and the third by Brigadier-General Charles Macgregor. Colonel Chapman, R.A., who had served in the same capacity with Sir Donald Stewart, was now Roberts' chief of staff. The marching out strength of the column was about 10,000 men, of whom 2835 were Europeans. Speed being an object and since the column might have to traverse rough ground, no wheeled artillery or transport accompanied it; the guns were carried on mules, the baggage was severely cut down, the supplies carried were reduced to a minimum, and the transport animals, numbering 8590, consisted of mules, ponies, and donkeys. It was known that the country could supply flour, sheep, and forage.

The time specified for the departure of the force from Sherpur was kept to the day. On the 8th the brigades moved out a short distance into camp, and on the following morning the march begun in earnest. The distance from Cabul to Candahar is about 320 miles, and the march naturally divides itself into three parts; from Cabul to Ghuznee, ninety-eight miles; from Ghuznee to Khelat-i-Ghilzai, one hundred and thirty-four miles; and from Khelat-i-Ghilzai to Candahar, eighty-eight miles, Ghuznee was reached on the seventh day, the daily average being fourteen miles— excellent work for troops unseasoned to long continuous travel, tramping steadily in a temperature of from 84° to 92° in the shade. When possible the force moved on a broad front, the brigades and regiments leading by rotation, and halts were made at specified intervals. The 'rouse' sounded at 2.45 A.M. and the march began at four; the troops were generally in camp by two P.M. and the baggage was usually reported all in by five; but the rearguard had both hard work and long hours. There was no sign of opposition anywhere, not a single load of baggage was left behind, comparatively few men fell out foot-sore, and the troops were steadily increasing in endurance and capacity of rapid and continuous marching.

At Ghuznee there was no rest day, and the steadfast dogged march was resumed on the morning of the 16th. The strain of this day's long tramp of twenty miles to Yergati was severe, but the men rallied gamely, and the General by dint of care and expedient was able to keep up the high pressure. 'The method,' writes General Chapman, 'of such marching as was now put in practice is not easy to describe; it combined the extreme of freedom in movement with carefully regulated halts, and the closest control in every portion of the column; it employed the individual intelligence of each man composing the masses in motion, and called on all for exertion in overcoming the difficulties of the march, in bearing its extraordinary toil, and in aiding the accomplishment of the object in view.' On the 20th a distance of twenty-one miles was covered—the longest day's march made; the effort was distressing owing to the heat and the lack of shade, but it was enforced by the absence of water. There was no relaxation in the rate of marching, and Khelat-i-Ghilzai was reached on the eighth day from Ghuznee, showing a daily average of nearly seventeen miles.

The 24th was a halt day at Khelat-i-Ghilzai, where Sir Frederick Roberts received a letter from General Primrose in Candahar, describing the sortie made on the village of Deh Khoja and giving details of his situation. It was resolved to evacuate Khelat-i-Ghilzai and take on its garrison with the column, which on the 25th resumed its march to Candahar. On his arrival at Tir Andaz on the following day the General found a letter from Candahar, informing him that at the news of the approach of the Cabul force Ayoub Khan had withdrawn from his investment of Candahar, and had shifted his camp to the village of Mazra in the Urgundab valley, nearly due north of Candahar. On the morning of the 27th General Hugh Gough was sent forward with two cavalry regiments a distance of thirty-four miles to Robat, the main column moving on to Khel Akhund, half way to the former place. Gough was accompanied by Captain Straton the principal signalling officer of the force, who was successful in communicating with Candahar, and in the afternoon Colonel St John, Major Leach, and Major Adam rode out to Robat, bringing the information that Ayoub Khan was engaged in strengthening his position in the Urgundab valley, and apparently had the intention to risk the issue of a battle. On the 28th the whole force was concentrated at Robat; and as it was desirable that the troops should reach Candahar fresh and ready for prompt action, the General decided to make the 20th a rest day and divide the nineteen miles from Robat to Candahar into two short marches.

The long forced march from Cabul may be regarded as having ended at Robat. The distance between those two places, 303 miles, had been covered in twenty days. It is customary in a long march to allow two rest days in each week, but Roberts had granted his force but a single rest day in the twenty days of its strenuous march. Including this rest day, the average daily march was a fraction over fifteen miles. As a feat of marching by a regular force of 10,000 men encumbered with baggage and followers, this achievement is unique, and it could have been accomplished only by thorough organisation and steady vigorous energy. Sir Frederick Roberts was so fortunate as to encounter no opposition. For this immunity he was indebted mainly to the stern lessons given to the tribesmen by Sir Donald Stewart at Ahmed Khel and Urzoo while that resolute soldier was marching from Candahar to Cabul, and in a measure also to the good offices of the new Ameer. But it must be remembered that Roberts had no assurance of exemption from hostile efforts to block his path, and that he marched ever ready to fight. It will long be remembered how when Roberts had started on the long swift march, the suspense as to its issue grew and swelled until the strain became intense. The safety of the garrison of Candahar was in grave hazard; the British prestige, impaired by the disaster of Maiwand, was trembling in the balance. The days passed, and there came no news of Roberts and of the 10,000 men with whom the wise, daring little chief had cut loose from any base and struck for his goal through a region of ill repute for fanaticism and bitter hostility. The pessimists among us held him to be rushing on his ruin. But Roberts marched light; he lived on what the country supplied; he gave the tribesmen no time to concentrate against him; and two days in advance of the time he had set himself he reached Candahar at the head of a force in full freshness of vigour and burning with zeal for immediate battle.

While halted at Robat on the 29th Sir Frederick heard

from General Phayre that his division had been retarded in its march by lack of transport, but that he hoped to have it assembled at Killa Abdoolla on the 28th, and would be able to move toward Candahar on the 30th. But as Killa Abdoolla is distant some eight marches from Candahar, it was obvious that General Phayre could not arrive in time to share in the impending battle. On the morning of the 31st the Cabul force reached Candahar. Sir Frederick Roberts, who had been suffering from fever for some days, was able to leave his dhooly and mount his horse in time to meet General Primrose and his officers to the east of Deh Khoja. The troops halted and breakfasted outside the Shikapore gate, while General Roberts entered the city and paid a visit to the Wali Shere Ali Khan. On his arrival he assumed command of the troops in Southern Afghanistan; and he remained resting in the city while the Cabul force marched to its selected camping ground near the destroyed cantonments on the north-west of Candahar. A few shots were fired, but the ground was occupied without opposition. Baker's brigade was on the right, camped in rear of Picquet hill, in the centre was Macpherson's brigade sheltered in its front by Karez hill, and on the left among orchards and enclosures was Macgregor's brigade, in rear of which was the cavalry.

CHAPTER 9

The Battle of Candahar

Although Yakoub Khan had ceased to beleaguer Candahar, he had withdrawn from that fortress but a very short distance, and the position he had taken up was of considerable strength. The Urgundab valley is separated on the north-west from the Candahar plain by a long precipitous spur trending south-west from the mountainous mass forming the eastern boundary of the valley further north. Where the spur quits the main range, due north of the city, the Murcha Pass affords communication between the Candahar plain and the Urgundab valley. The spur, its summit serrated by alternate heights and depressions, is again crossed lower down by an easy pass known as the Babawali Kotul. It is continued beyond this saddle for about a mile, still maintaining its south-westerly trend, never losing its precipitous character, and steeply scarped on its eastern face; and it finally ends in the plain in a steep descent of several hundred feet. The section of it from the Babawali Kotul to its south-western termination is known as the Pir Paimal hill, from a village of that name in the valley near its extremity. Ayoub Khan had made his camp near the village of Mazra, behind the curtain formed by the spur described, and about a mile higher up in the valley than the point at which the spur is crossed by the road over the Babawali Kotul. He was thus, with that point artificially strengthened and defended by artillery, well protected against a direct attack from the direction of Candahar, and was exposed only to the risk of a turning movement round the extremity of the Pir Paimal hill. Such a movement might be made the reverse of easy. A force advancing to attempt it must do so exposed to fire from the commanding summit of the Pir Paimal; around the base of that elevation there were several plain villages, and an expanse of enclosed orchards and gardens which strongly held were capable of stubborn defence. In the valley behind the Pir Paimal hill there was the lofty detached Kharoti hill, the fire from which would meet in the teeth a force essaying the turning movement; and the interval between the two hills, through which was the access to the Mazra camps, was obstructed by deep irrigation channels whose banks afforded cover for defensive fire, and could be swept by a cross fire from the hills on either flank.

Sir Frederick Roberts at a glance had perceived that a direct attack by the Babawali Kotul must involve very heavy loss, and he resolved on the alternative of turning the Afghan position. A reconnaissance was made on the afternoon of the 31st by General Gough, accompanied by Colonel Chapman. He penetrated to within a short distance of the village of Pir Paimal, where it was ascertained that the enemy were strongly entrenched, and where several guns were unmasked. A great deal of valuable information was obtained before the enemy began to interfere with the leisurely withdrawal. The cavalry suffered little, but the Sikh infantry covering the retirement of the reconnaissance were hard pressed by great masses of Afghan regulars and irregulars. So boldly did the enemy come on that the third and part of the first brigade came into action, and the firing did not cease until the evening. The enemy were clearly in the belief that the reconnaissance was an advance in force which they had been able to check and indeed drive in, and they were opportunely audacious in the misapprehension that they had gained a success. The information brought in decided the General to attack on the following morning; and having matured his dispositions, he explained them personally to the commanding officers in the early morning of September 1st. The plan of attack was perfectly simple. The Babawali Kotul was to be plied with a brisk cannonade and threatened by demonstrations both of cavalry and infantry; while the first and second brigades, with the third in reserve, were to turn the extremity of the Pir Paimal hill, force the enemy's right in the interval between that hill and the Kharoti eminence, take in reverse the Babawali Kotul, and pressing on up the Urgundab valley, carry Ayoub Khan's principal camp at Mazra. The Bombay cavalry brigade was to watch the roads over the Murcha and Babawali Kotuls, supported by infantry and artillery belonging to General Primrose's command, part of which was also detailed for the protection of the city; and to hold the ground from which the Cabul brigades were to advance. General Gough was to take the cavalry of the Cabul column across the Urgundab, so as to reach by a wide circuit the anticipated line of the Afghan retreat.

Soon after nine A.M. the forty-pounders on the right of Picquet hill began a vigorous cannonade of the Babawali Kotul, which was sturdily replied to by the three field-guns the enemy had in battery on that elevation. It had been early apparent that the Ayoub's army was in great heart, and apparently meditating an offensive movement had moved out so far into the plain as to occupy the villages of Mulla Sahibdad opposite the British right, and Gundigan on the left front of the British left. Both villages were right in the fair way of Roberts' intended line of advance; they, the adjacent enclosures, and the interval between the villages were strongly held, and manifestly the first thing to be done was to force the enemy back from those advanced positions. Two batteries opened a heavy shell fire on the Sahibdad village, under cover of which Macpherson advanced his brigade against it, the 2nd Goorkhas and 92nd Highlanders in his first line. Simultaneously Baker moved out to the assault of Gundigan, clearing the gardens and orchards between him and that village, and keeping touch as he advanced with the first brigade.

The shell fire compelled the Afghan occupants of Sahibdad to lie close, and it was not until they were near the village that Macpherson's two leading regiments encountered much opposition. It was carried at the bayonet point after a very stubborn resistance; the place was full of ghazees who threw their lives away recklessly, and continued to fire on the British soldiers from houses and cellars after the streets had been cleared. The 92d lost several men, but the Afghans were severely punished; it was reported that 200 were killed in this village alone. While a detachment remained to clear out the village, the brigade under a heavy fire from the slopes and crest of the Pir Paimal hill moved on in the direction of that hill's south-western extremity, the progress of the troops impeded by obstacles in the shape of dry water-cuts, orchards, and walled enclosures, every yard of which was infested by enemies and had to be made good by steady fighting.

While Macpherson was advancing on Sahibdad, Baker's brigade had been pushing on through complicated lanes and walled enclosures toward the village of Gundigan. The opposition experienced was very resolute. The Afghans held their ground behind loopholed walls which had to be carried by storm, and they did not hesitate to take the offensive by making vigorous counter-rushes. Baker's two leading regiments were the 72d and the 2d Sikhs. The left

wing of the former supported by the 5th Goorkhas, the old
and tried comrades of the 72d, assailed and took the village.
Its right wing fought its way through the orchards between
it and Sahibdad, in the course of which work it came under
a severe enfilading fire from a loopholed wall which the
Sikhs on the right were attempting to turn. Captain Frome
and several men had been struck down and the hot fire
had staggered the Highlanders, when their chief, Colonel
Brownlow, came up on foot. That gallant soldier gave the
word for a rush, but immediately fell mortally wounded.
After much hard fighting Baker's brigade got forward into
opener country, but was then exposed to the fire of an
Afghan battery near the extremity of the Pir Paimal spur,
and to the attacks of great bodies of ghazees, which were
withstood stoutly by the Sikhs and driven off by a bayonet
attack delivered by the Highlanders.

The two brigades had accomplished the first part of
their task. They were now in alignment with each other;
and the work before them was to accomplish the turning movement round the steep extremity of the Pir Paimal
ridge. Macpherson's brigade, hugging the face of the elevation, brought up the left shoulder and having accomplished
the turning movement, swept up the valley and carried the
village of Pir Paimal by a series of rushes. Here, however,
Major White commanding the advance of the 92d, found
himself confronted by great masses of the enemy, who appeared determined to make a resolute stand about their
guns which were in position south-west of the Babawali
Kotul. Reinforcements were observed hurrying up from
Ayoub's standing camp at Mazra, and the Afghan guns on
the Kotul had been reversed so that their fire should enfilade
the British advance. Discerning that in such circumstances
prompt action was imperative, Macpherson determined to
storm the position without waiting for reinforcements. The

The Battle of Candahar

92d under Major White led the way, covered by the fire
of a field battery and supported by the 5th Goorkhas and
the 23d Pioneers. Springing out of a watercourse at the
challenge of their leader, the Highlanders rushed across the
open ground. The Afghans, sheltered by high banks, fired
steadily and well; their riflemen from the Pir Paimal slopes
poured in a sharp cross fire; their guns were well served.
But the Scottish soldiers were not to be denied. Their losses
were severe, but they took the guns at the point of the bayonet, and valiantly supported by the Goorkhas and pioneers,
shattered and dispersed the mass of Afghans, which was
reckoned to have numbered some 8000 men. No chance
was given the enemy to rally. They were headed off from
the Pir Paimal slopes by Macpherson. Baker hustled them
out of cover in the watercourses in the basin on the left,
and while one stream of fugitives poured away across the
river, another rolled backward into and through Ayoub's
camp at Mazra.

While Macpherson had effected his turning movement
close under the ridge, Baker's troops on the left had to make
a wider sweep before bringing up the left shoulder and
wheeling into the hollow between the Pir Paimal and the
Kharoti hill. They swept out of their path what opposition
they encountered, and moved up the centre of the hollow,
where their commander halted them until Macpherson's
brigade on the right, having accomplished its more arduous
work, should come up and restore the alignment. Baker had
sent Colonel Money with a half battalion away to the left
to take possession of the Kharoti hill, where he found and
captured three Afghan guns. Pressing toward the northern
end of the hill, Money to his surprise found himself in full
view of Ayoub's camp, which was then full of men and in
rear of which a line of cavalry was drawn up. Money was
too weak to attack alone and sent to General Baker for

reinforcements which, however, could not be spared him, and the gallant Money had perforce to remain looking on while the advance of Macpherson and Baker caused the evacuation of Ayoub's camp and the flight of his cavalry and infantry toward the Urgundab. But the discovery and capture of five more Afghan cannon near Babawali village was some consolation for the enforced inaction.

Considerable numbers of Ayoub's troops had earlier pushed through the Babawali Pass, and moved down toward the right front of General Burrows' Bombay brigade in position about Picquet hill. Having assured himself that Burrows was able to hold his own, Sir Frederick Roberts ordered Macgregor to move the third brigade forward toward Pir Paimal village, whither he himself rode. On his arrival there he found that the first and second brigades were already quite a mile in advance. The battle really had already been won but there being no open view to the front General Ross, who commanded the whole infantry division, had no means of discerning this result; and anticipating the likelihood that Ayoub's camp at Mazra would have to be taken by storm, he halted the brigades to replenish ammunition. This delay gave opportunity for the entire evacuation of the Afghan camp, which when reached without any further opposition and entered at one P.M. was found to be deserted. The tents had been left standing; 'all the rude equipage of a half barbarous army had been abandoned—the meat in the cooking pots, the bread half kneaded in the earthen vessels, the bazaar with its ghee pots, dried fruits, flour, and corn.' Ayoub's great marquee had been precipitately abandoned, and the fine carpets covering its floor were left. But in the hurry of their flight the Afghans had found time to illustrate their barbarity by murdering their prisoner Lieutenant Maclaine, whose body was found near Ayoub's tent with the throat cut. To this deed Ayoub does not seem to have been

163

privy. The sepoys who were prisoners with Maclaine testified that Ayoub fled about eleven o'clock, leaving the prisoners in charge of the guard with no instructions beyond a verbal order that they were not to be killed. It was more than an hour later when the guard ordered the unfortunate officer out of his tent and took his life.

The victory was complete and Ayoub's army was in full rout. Unfortunately no cavalry were in hand for a pursuit from the Mazra camp. The scheme for intercepting the fugitive Afghans by sending the cavalry brigade on a wide movement across the Urgundab, and striking the line of their probable retreat toward the Khakrez valley, may have been ingenious in conception, but in practice did not have the desired effect. But Ayoub had been decisively beaten. He had lost the whole of his artillery numbering thirty-two pieces, his camp, an immense quantity of ammunition, about 1000 men killed; his army was dispersed, and he himself was a fugitive with a mere handful along with him of the army of 12,000 men whom he had commanded in the morning.

The battle of Candahar was an effective finale to the latest of our Afghan wars, and it is in this sense that it is chiefly memorable. The gallant men who participated in the winning of it must have been the first to smile at the epithets of 'glorious' and 'brilliant' which were lavished on the victory. In truth, if it had not been a victory our arms would have sustained a grave discredit. The soldiers of Roberts and Stewart had been accustomed to fight and to conquer against heavy numerical odds, which were fairly balanced by their discipline and the superiority of their armament. But in the battle of Candahar the numerical disparity was non-existent, and Ayoub had immensely the disadvantage as regarded trained strength. His force according to the reckoning ascertained by the British general, amounted all told to 12,800 men. The strength of the British force, not including the detail of Bombay troops garrisoning Candahar, was over 12,000. But this army 12,000 strong, consisted entirely of disciplined soldiers of whom over one-fifth were Europeans. The accepted analysis of Ayoub's army shows it to have consisted of 4000 regular infantry, 800 regular cavalry, 5000 tribal irregular infantry of whom an indefinite proportion was no doubt ghazees, and 3000 irregular horsemen. In artillery strength the two forces were nearly equal. When it is remembered that Charasiah was won by some 2500 soldiers of whom only about 800 were Europeans, contending against 10,000 Afghans in an exceptionally strong position and well provided with artillery, Sir Frederick Roberts' wise decision to make assurance doubly sure in dealing with Ayoub at Candahar stands out very strikingly. Perforce in his battles around Cabul he had taken risks, but because those adventures had for the most part been successful he was not the man to weaken the certainty of an all-important issue by refraining from putting into the field every soldier at his disposal. And he was wisely cautious in his tactics. That he was strong enough to make a direct attack by storming the Babawali Kotul and the Pir Paimal hill was clear in the light of previous experience. But if there was more 'brilliancy' in a direct attack, there was certain to be heavier loss than would be incurred in the less dashing turning movement, and Sir Frederick with the true spirit of a commander chose the more artistic and less bloody method of earning his victory. It did not cost him dear. His casualties of the day were thirty-six killed including three officers, and 218 wounded among whom were nine officers.

The battle of Candahar brought to a close the latest of our Afghan wars. Sir Frederick Roberts quitted Candahar on the 9th September, and marched to Quetta with part of his division. On the 15th October, at Sibi, he resigned his command, and taking sick leave to England sailed from Bombay on the 30th October. His year of hard and successful service in Afghanistan greatly enhanced his reputation as a prompt, skilful, and enterprising soldier.

The Pisheen and Sibi valleys are the sole tangible results remaining to us of the two campaigns in Afghanistan sketched in these volumes—campaigns which cost the lives of many gallant men slain in action or dead of disease, and involved the expenditure of about twenty millions sterling. Lord Beaconsfield's vaunted 'scientific frontier,' condemned by a consensus of the best military opinions, was rejected by the Liberal Government which had recently acceded to power, whose decision was that both the Khyber Pass and the Kuram valley should be abandoned. On this subject Sir Frederick Roberts wrote with great shrewdness:

> We have nothing to fear from Afghanistan, and the best thing to do is to leave it as much as possible to itself. It may not be very flattering to our *amour propre*, but I feel sure I am right when I say that the less the Afghans see of us the less they will dislike us. Should Russia in future years attempt to conquer Afghanistan, or invade India through it, we should have a better chance of attaching the Afghans to our interest if we avoid all interference with them in the meantime.'

During the winter of 1880-1 the Khyber and the Kuram were evacuated by the British troops, the charge of keeping open and quiet the former being entrusted to tribal levies paid by the Indian Government.

So far, then, as regarded the north-western frontier, the status quo ante had been fallen back upon. But there was a keen difference of opinion in regard to the disposition of the salient angle furnished by Candahar. Throughout the

British occupation and the negotiations with Abdurrah-man, the annexation of Candahar had been consistently repudiated. The intention on our part announced was to separate it from Cabul, and to place it under the independent rule of a Barakzai prince. Such a prince had actually been appointed in Shere Ali Khan, and although that incompetent Sirdar was wise enough to abdicate a position for which he was not strong enough, this action did not relieve us from our pledges against annexation. Nevertheless many distinguished men whose opinions were abstractly entitled to weight, were strongly in favour of our retention of Candahar. Among those were the late Lord Napier of Magdala, Sir Henry Rawlinson, Sir Edward Hamley, Sir Donald Stewart, and Sir Frederick Roberts. Among the authorities opposed to the occupation of Candahar were such men as the late Lord Lawrence and General Charles Gordon, Sir Robert Montgomery, Lord Wolseley, Sir Henry Norman, Sir John Adye, and Sir Archibald Alison.

While the professional experts differed and while the 'Candahar debates' in Parliament were vehement and prolonged, the issue, assuming that fidelity to pledges was still regarded as a national virtue, was perfectly clear and simple. In the frank words of Sir Lepel Griffin: 'We could not have remained in Candahar without a breach of faith.' And he added with unanswerable force: 'Our withdrawal was in direct accordance with the reiterated and solemn professions which I had been instructed to make, and the assurances of the Government of India to the chiefs and people of Cabul.... The wisdom of the policy of retiring from Candahar may be a fair matter for argument, but it was one on which both Governments were agreed. I am convinced that withdrawal, after our public assurances, was the only practicable policy.'

Lord Ripon acted on his instructions 'to keep in view

the paramount importance of effecting a withdrawal from Candahar on the earliest suitable occasion.' The abdication of the Wali Shere Ali Khan cleared the air to some extent. A British garrison under the command of General Hume wintered in Candahar. Ayoub Khan was a competitor for the rulership of the southern province, but he received no encouragement, and after some negotiation the Ameer Abdurrahman was informed that Candahar was reincorporated with the kingdom of Afghanistan, and it was intimated to him that the capital would be given over to the Governor, accompanied by a suitable military force, whom he should send. On the 1st of April an Afghan force entered Candahar, followed presently by Mahomed Hassan Khan, the Governor nominated by the Ameer. General Hume soon after marched out, and after halting for a time in the Pisheen valley to watch the course of events in Candahar, he continued his march toward India. The restless Ayoub did not tamely submit to the arrangement which gave Candahar to Abdurrahman. Spite of many arduous difficulties, spite of lack of money and of mutinous troops, he set out toward Candahar in July 1881. Mahomed Hassan marched against him from Candahar, and a battle was fought at Maiwand on the anniversary of the defeat of General Burrows on the same field. Ayoub was the conqueror, and he straightway took possession of the capital and was for the time ruler of the province. But Abdurrahman, subsidised with English money and English arms, hurried from Cabul, encountered Ayoub outside the walls of Candahar, and inflicted on him a decisive defeat. His flight to Herat was followed up, he sustained a second reverse there, and took refuge in Persia. Abdurrahman's tenure of the Cabul sovereignty had been at first extremely precarious; but he proved a man at once strong, resolute, and politic. In little more than a year after his accession he was ruler of Shere Ali's Afghanistan; Candahar and Herat had both come to him, and that without very serious exertion. He continues to reign quietly, steadfastly, and firmly; and there never has been any serious friction between him and the Government of India, whose wise policy is a studied abstinence from interference in the internal affairs of the Afghan kingdom.

[At the time of publication of this book British soldiers are once again serving in Afghanistan. *The Leonaur Editors*]

LEONAUR

ALSO FROM LEONAUR

AVAILABLE IN SOFTCOVER OR HARDCOVER WITH DUST JACKET

CAPTAIN OF THE 95th (Rifles) *by Jonathan Leach*—An officer of Wellington's Sharpshooters during the Peninsular, South of France and Waterloo Campaigns of the Napoleonic Wars.

THE KHAKEE RESSALAH *by Robert Henry Wallace Dunlop*—Service & adventure with the Meerut volunteer horse during the Indian mutiny 1857-1858

BUGLER AND OFFICER OF THE RIFLES *by William Green & Harry Smith* With the 95th (Rifles) during the Peninsular & Waterloo Campaigns of the Napoleonic Wars

BAYONETS, BUGLES AND BONNETS *by James 'Thomas' Todd*—Experiences of hard soldiering with the 71st Foot - the Highland Light Infantry - through many battles of the Napoleonic wars including the Peninsular & Waterloo Campaigns

A NORFOLK SOLDIER IN THE FIRST SIKH WAR *by J W Baldwin*—Experiences of a private of H.M. 9th Regiment of Foot in the battles for the Punjab, India 1845-46

A CAVALRY OFFICER DURING THE SEPOY REVOLT *by A.R.D. Mackenzie*—Experiences with the 3rd Bengal Light Cavalry, the Guides and Sikh Irregular Cavalry from the outbreak to Delhi and Lucknow

THE ADVENTURES OF A LIGHT DRAGOON *by George Farmer & G.R. Gleig*—A cavalryman during the Peninsular & Waterloo Campaigns, in captivity & at the siege of Bhurtpore, India

THE COMPLEAT RIFLEMAN HARRIS *by Benjamin Harris as told to & transcribed by Captain Henry Curling*—The adventures of a soldier of the 95th (Rifles) during the Peninsular Campaign of the Napoleonic Wars

THE RED DRAGOON *by W.J. Adams*—With the 7th Dragoon Guards in the Cape of Good Hope against the Boers & the Kaffir tribes during the 'war of the axe' 1843-48

THE LIFE OF THE REAL BRIGADIER GERARD - Volume 1 - THE YOUNG HUSSAR 1782 - 1807 *by Jean-Baptiste De Marbot*—A French Cavalryman Of the Napoleonic Wars at Marengo, Austerlitz, Jena, Eylau & Friedland

THE LIFE OF THE REAL BRIGADIER GERARD Volume 2 IMPERIAL AIDE-DE-CAMP 1807 - 1811 *by Jean-Baptiste De Marbot*—A French Cavalryman of the Napoleonic Wars at Saragossa, Landshut, Eckmuhl, Ratisbon, Aspern-Essling, Wagram, Busaco & Torres Vedras

Lightning Source UK Ltd.
Milton Keynes UK
09 December.2010

164082UK00001B/105/A